Table of Contents

Introduction 3
Running journal 8
Chapter 1: Understanding the body to maximize the benefits of your training efforts 11
    What is supercompensation? 11
    The bodies energy systems 15
    Weight 17
Chapter 2: Recovery 19
    How do you know if you are recovered? 19
    Recovery during the day 19
    Breathing while running 31
Chapter 3: Training load 33
    Heart rate 33
    Experiences 39
Chapter 4: Exercises to remain injury free 42
    Preventing knee, calf and achilles injuries 42
    Preventing shin, calf and Achilles injuries 51
    Proposed workouts 57
Chapter 5: Theory of the training schedules 59
    Training based on heart rate 61
    Interval training 62
    Why do other runners do very long runs 64
    Training schedules explained 67
    Training on marathon heart rate 70

What are the disadvantages of the proposed schedule? 72

Which training schedule should you follow? 74

Chapter 6: Marathon schedule 76

    Nutrition for the marathon 82

    Interval Pace 84

    Marathon Heart rate 85

Chapter 7: Half Marathon schedule 171

    Nutrition for the half marathon 180

    Interval Pace 182

    Half marathon Heart rate 183

Chapter 8: 10K schedule 269

    Interval Pace 274

Chapter 9: Beginner schedules 276

    Schedule Beginner 5K 283

    Training schedule for beginners that want to lose weight before they can run injury free 287

Epilogue 293

References 294

Introduction

You want results, and you want them fast. You can achieve all your fitness goals by running less than you ever thought was possible. What if I told you that you only need to run three times a week. Run by Heart Rate's unique training approach is suited for every experience level. The unique approach limits the risk of overtraining and substantially cuts the risk of injury while producing faster race times. The key feature of the detailed training plans for the 5K, 10K, half-marathon, and marathon is the "Run by Heart Rate" approach, which consists of:

3–4 quality runs, including an aerobic easy-speed workout below your anaerobic heart rate threshold, two runs at your race-specific heart rate, and a recovery run. This approach improves your endurance, running economy, and running speed. Training at a specific heart rate will allow you to achieve an optimal training effect, ensuring your performance will get better over time. Even if you want to run a marathon, you will only run four times a week. Moreover, the longest training run in the Run by Heart Rate marathon schedule is only 14K (9 miles)! This allows you to keep doing the things you love while still getting the results you want.

I've written this book together with my coach. We were both trained in the principles of Klaas Lok. Klaas Lok is the author of the easy interval method and was one of the best Dutch athletes of his time. The easy interval method is a great training approach but is more suited to track runners (although it can also work for longer runs). We have taken the best of this schedule and combined it with a very popular schedule by Sportrusten. Sportrusten's approach suits all types of long-distance runners, from 5Ks to marathons. The training schedule by Sportrusten has been very successful but lacks speed workouts to improve your running economy and speed. The combination of these training schedules is the best of both worlds.

If you want to find out more about the easy interval method visit https://easyintervalmethod.com/ , If you want to find out more about Sportrusten visit https://www.bol.com/nl/nl/p/de-hardloaprevolutie/9200000103547971/?bltgh=nXShs1-8aW0laGu0a1RGGg.2_16.18.ProductTitle

So how do you get the best results as soon as possible? Supercompensation is the methodology and training adaptation that gets you there. In short, it is the optimal balance between training and recovery. By following the schedules in this book, you will achieve supercompensation, whereas with other regular training schedules, you will not. I have described several training schedules that you can follow, depending on your current level and your current goals. The training schedules range from not being able to run at all to training for a marathon. Even if you have never run before, you will be able to run at least 5 kilometers (3.10 miles) in just 100 days.

Striking a perfect balance between exercise and recovery is also a cornerstone for losing weight. And by following the training schedules described, you will finally discover the sweet spot. Moreover, the training sessions are not like many other exercise programs, where you give it your all, experience physical torture to make progress, and feel sore and tired every day. Instead, with these training schedules, you will feel better after a workout instead of worse.

To give you a first glimpse of the difference between the training schedules in this book and regular schedules, I will compare the Run by Heart Rate marathon training schedule to a traditional marathon training schedule.

I have looked at several popular training schedules for the marathon, and many of them are similar to the schedule on RunnersWeb.com.

The RunnersWeb schedule starts with six training days, and the longest run is 16 kilometers (9.94 miles). There is also an hour of cross-training in between. Immediately in week 1, you train five times and run 42 kilometers (26 miles), and you do another sport for an hour! That is already more than you would do with the Run By Heart Rates marathon training schedule in the toughest week. In Run by Heart Rate's toughest week, you will run four times: twice, 14 kilometers (9 miles); once, a speed workout of 9 kilometers (5 miles); and once, a recovery run of 7 kilometers (4 miles), totaling 44 kilometers (27 miles). Compare this to RunnersWeb's toughest week, and the difference in mileage is huge: 76 kilometers (47.22 miles) compared to Run by Heart Rate's toughest week with 44 kilometers (27 miles).

What is particularly striking about the regular training plans is that long-distance endurance training is regularly followed by even longer-distance training immediately the following week. For example, in week 10, you train 70 kilometers (43.49 miles) in total, and the longest distance you train is 30 kilometers (18.64 miles). A week later, you train 76 kilometers (47.22 miles) in total, and the longest training is 32 kilometers (19.88 miles).

It scared me just by reading it. I would not think about running 30 kilometers (18.64 miles) on Sunday and then training for 76 kilometers (47.22 miles) again the following week, including an endurance run of 32 kilometers. When does the body have time to recover? Never!! This will also put you at high risk for developing injuries, and most likely you will not even finish the training plan. This excessive mileage occurs not only with marathon training plans but also with beginner training plans for people who want to run their first 5K or 10K race.

Imagine the daily lives of people following regular schedules. Their days must revolve around running, making it no longer fun. By following the schedules in this book, running doesn't have to interfere with your everyday life. If you want to run a marathon, your maximum training distance will be 14 kilometers (8.69 miles). So you can spend the rest of your time doing the things you love while still achieving all the goals you're after and improving your personal best times!

Appreciation notes

First of all, I would like to send my appreciation to Kneesovertoesguy, for relieving me of knee injuries, shin splints, and the pain of an old torn Achilles. Allowing me to run a marathon. I'm a massive fan, and I hope this e-book inspires others to use his wisdom as well. Many of his exercises that you can find on his Instagram are described in this book.

I would also like to send my appreciation to Klaas Lok and Sportrusten. As both approaches are successful and have inspired many people to start running.

I would also like to thank my girlfriend for putting up with all my talk about running and supporting me by cycling next to me during many workouts in the past few years.

Running journal

As the runs accumulate it becomes increasingly difficult to remember how far you have come along your running journey. I've created a running journal that allows you to capture this incredible journey. Inspiring you to keep going forward and achieve new goals. It consists of 1 goals page, 3 pages reserved for your records, 2 pages for race registrations, 4 pages to record your race results, and 98 pages to track 196 runs!

I've created two running journals one in black and one in pink running.

Black: https://www.amazon.com/dp/B09B38BT4K

Pink: https://www.amazon.com/dp/B09919JWS5 Running

Journal for men: Good things come to those who run.

Running journal for women: Good things come to those who run

Chapter 1: Understanding the body to maximize the benefits of your training efforts

We want results, and we want them fast. So how do we get the best results as soon as possible? Supercompensation is the methodology and training adaptation that gets you there. Achieving supercompensation is the main goal of any training schedule, and understanding supercompensation is critical to becoming faster and running farther than ever before.

What is supercompensation?

Our bodies are great at responding to the stress we apply. Look at bodybuilders who sculpt their muscles by lifting weights and applying the needed stimulus to grow muscles. If you apply the training stimulus with the proper structure, the body responds to that stress, increasing (an)aerobic capabilities and/or strength. Sounds good, but what exactly is supercompensation and how does one obtain it?

Many of us see the term "supercompensation" as daunting as if it's associated with an extremely rigorous and demanding training process that's risky and should be avoided. That is wrong.

Supercompensation as a model

Supercompensation is a process that can be broken down into several phases, which are shown in the figure just below the description of the four phases.

- Phase 1: Training: An athlete begins to introduce a training stimulus that's higher than what the body is previously used to. This stress prompts fatigue which is reflected in declining performance.
- Phase 2 : Recovery: Declining performance leaves an athlete with no choice but to introduce recovery in

some form. That can be active rest, active recovery sessions, or simply taking a day off completely. Proper recovery and nutrition allow energy and performance to return to the original baseline fitness level.
- Phase 3: Supercompensation: After adequate recovery from a workload your body was previously not suited to, the responsive nature of the body builds itself in anticipation of the next expected challenge. You've tricked your body into becoming suitable to withstand the next effort based on the previously experienced challenge in phase one.
- Phase 4: Decline of fitness: Naturally, all good things come to an end. When no new training stimulus is applied, fitness declines.

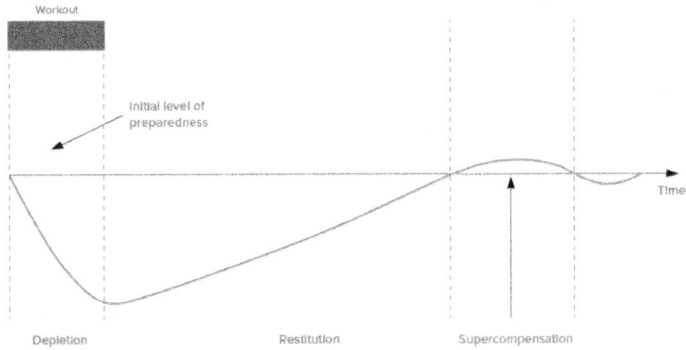

Preparedness is continually depleted due to training stress, then restituted through recovery

The supercompensation effect

The supercompensation effect

Your fitness is never stagnant. You are either increasing fitness or decreasing fitness. Timing your training and applying the proper training load are critical to taking advantage of and allowing supercompensation to take place. This determines whether the new training stimulus will further increase or decrease your fitness. All training programs will incorporate an increase in training load while making sure you recover well, to take full advantage of supercompensation. As shown in the figure below, the fitness level eventually spirals upward.

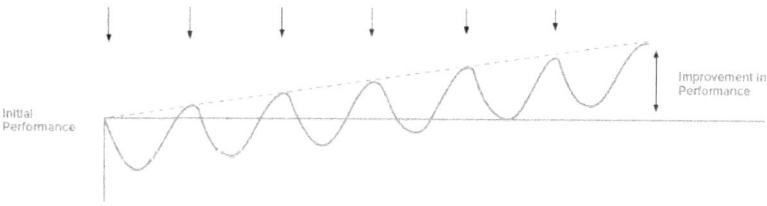

Preparedness is continually depleted due to training stress, then restituted through recovery. As time moves on, performance increases. This is often called the train-recover-train cycle.

"Declining fitness levels"

If you train too hard or rest too little, you run the risk of overtraining, especially when dealing with consecutive high-intensity workouts.

In the instance of nonfunctional overreaching, adequate recovery hasn't allowed your fitness to surpass your previous level of fitness before training is reintroduced, or you've reached a peak level of fitness yet continued to apply a hefty dose of training without allowing adequate recovery. The result? A gradual decline in fitness and lack of ability to perform.

If left unaddressed, this could lead to overtraining. Overtraining is no joke, this can end your season, requiring up to a multi-month recovery. Large changes in resting heart rate, extreme fatigue, and/or apathy for the sport are all indications of non-functional overreaching, which is a sign to take it easy.

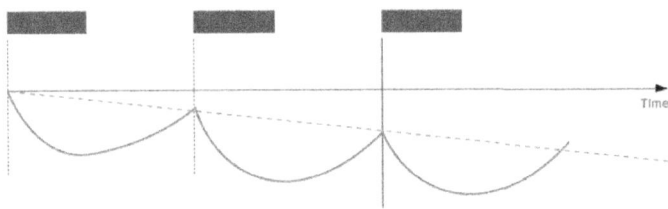

Preparedness is continually driven down due to unrelenting training stress. The period of compensation in recovery is cut short, creating no opportunity for supercompensation effects.

Detraining

I keep mentioning this window your training should be framed within to achieve supercompensation. You can train too early, but you can also train too late.

Say you reach the peak of supercompensation but don't train during this window. The training stress that moves you into the new cycle of supercompensation is missing, and fitness begins to drop off. Keeping a consistent pattern in your training is the only way to avoid the risk of detraining. You can see this in the figure below.

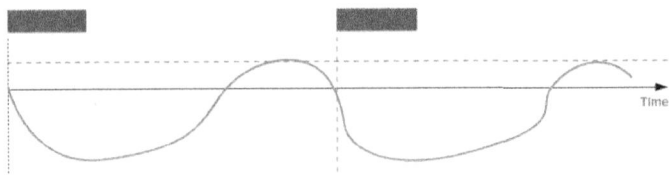

The training stimulus is introduced too late, leaving no chance to take hold of supercompensation effects.

How do you achieve supercompensation?

In this book, you will discover personal training schedules that apply the appropriate training load, and you will discover how to improve your recovery. This will spiral your performance upward due to the benefits of supercompensation.

The bodies energy systems

To increase your performance, I think it is best to have a basic understanding of the body's energy system. A marathon runner will use a different energy system than a sprinter. So the goal you set will also determine what training activities you should do to increase your performance. The body has two energy systems: aerobic and anaerobic. But what is the difference?

Every movement we make requires energy; there are two main ways that this is done, one with oxygen and one without oxygen.

Aerobic means "with air" and refers to the body producing energy with the use of oxygen. This typically involves any exercise that lasts longer than two minutes in duration. Continuous steady-state exercise, like long-distance running, is performed aerobically. During this type of exercise, the body can mostly use fat as fuel. As the training intensity increases, more carbohydrates are used as fuel.

Anaerobic means "without air" and refers to the body producing energy without using oxygen. The anaerobic energy system is also called the lactic acid system. Primarily using carbohydrates as fuel, this energy system powers the muscles anywhere from ten to thirty seconds for intense efforts, like sprinting. The anaerobic system bypasses the use of oxygen to create ATP quickly through glycolysis. But this speed comes at a cost; its energy production is limited due to excess byproducts.

The most important byproduct of this process is lactate. Some of the excess lactate enters the Krebs cycle for aerobic respiration, and the rest is cleared via the bloodstream. As your effort becomes more intense, the amount of lactate eventually outpaces the body's ability to use and clear it. This balance point is referred to as the lactate threshold; this is an important term, and you will discover more about it.

You can notice this when you run, as you experience pain and burning sensations in your legs because the anaerobic process creates acidity in the muscles.

What is aerobic capacity?
*A widely used measure for aerobic capacity is maximal aerobic capacity, also known as VO2 max. VO2 max is a measurement of the maximal amount of oxygen your body can effectively consume.

As exercise intensity rises, your muscles use more and more oxygen to fuel aerobic metabolism. Eventually, the muscular demand for oxygen outpaces the cardiovascular system's ability to deliver it. Any increase in workload beyond this point is fueled anaerobically and is only briefly sustainable.

VO2 max is an important determinant of ability in endurance sports. The higher your VO2 max, the greater your capacity to take in and utilize oxygen.

VO2 max can be expressed in two ways. Absolute VO2 max refers to the number of liters of oxygen used per minute (L/min) and measures total O2 consumption. The average is around 2.5 liters per minute for the untrained man and around 2 liters per minute for the untrained woman. Relative VO2 max includes body weight in the calculation and is defined as milliliters of oxygen consumed per kilogram of body weight per minute (mL/kg/min). Relative VO2 max values are most commonly used in sports, and I will use them in this book. On average, the relative VO2 max of an untrained man is 40–45 mL/kg/min and closer to 30-35 mL/kg/min for an untrained woman. The relative

VO2 max largely determines how fast you can run a certain distance. Race times for events can be predicted by relative VO2 max, as shown in the table below for the 5K.

Relative VO2 max	Predicted 5K time
85	12.39
80	13.38
75	14.44
70	16.01
65	17.29
60	19.12
55	21.14
50	23.40
45	26.38
40	30.19
35	33.59

What is anaerobic Capacity?

As with all of your energy systems, the anaerobic system has its limitations. Anaerobic capacity is measured in power output during a thirty-second sprint test. Alongside capacity, another important metric is repeatability—how many times you can repeat a hard effort. Both are crucial for performance.

Weight

As you previously discovered, relative VO2 max is a good predictor of race times. Relative VO2 max also incorporates weight. If you manage to lose weight, your relative VO2 max will increase, and you can expect to run faster when you drop weight. For example, one of the athletes I trained had a relative VO2 max of 44.41. But at that time, she liked to eat fast food and drink wine. She managed to drop 10 kg, and her estimated relative VO2 max increased to 51.24. When she did a 10K race, she ran 10 minutes faster than her previous personal best. Her estimated marathon time even dropped by a whopping 50 minutes. Even the best training schedule would have a hard time increasing performance by this much.

Thus if you have weight to lose then losing weight is a good way to become faster.

Chapter 2: Recovery

The effects of supercompensation are crucial for improvement, and knowing when to train and when to rest is vital to achieving supercompensation. In this chapter, I will focus on recovery. This is easily the most overlooked part of increasing performance, but it is vital to spiraling your performance upwards.

How do you know if you are recovered?

A good way to know if you are recovered from a training session is to compare your resting heart rate in the morning after a training session to your resting heart rate on a fully rested day. I advise you to measure your heart rate every day. During the first week, you measure your resting heart rate without exercising to be able to measure your well-rested resting heart rate.

If your resting heart rate is higher than +/- 5 beats compared to a well-rested day, it is unwise to train intensively. You have two options at this point: train less intensely or don't train that day. My resting heart rate is 48; if my resting heart rate is above 53–54, I will either go for an easy run or train the next day.

How can you measure your resting heart rate?

I like to measure my resting heart rate when I am just awake. Be sure to stick to a specific moment during the day, as you would also do when you measure your weight. Because it is important to keep out variations that are not due to the training load. You can measure your resting heart rate by simply counting your heartbeat for 30 seconds and multiplying this by 2. Nowadays, I use my Garmin Forerunner 245 to determine my resting heart rate.

Recovery during the day

Recovery takes place right after the training activity. The quality of recovery is largely dependent on the state of the body. The body needs to be relaxed to recover well. Furthermore, food and sleep are also important. But most of all, breathing during the day appears to be critical for the body to be relaxed and recover after training.

What is normal breathing?

Let us start with medical norms for breathing. Normal breathing is regular, invisible (no chest or belly movements), and inaudible (no panting, no wheezing, no sighing, no yawning, no sneezing, no coughing, and no deep inhalations or exhalations) with a closed mouth. The official medical norm for ventilation is about 6 l/min (liters of air per minute). The main function of breathing is to control concentrations of two gases: CO_2 and O_2. The corresponding CP is 40, later in this chapter, you will discover what CP is.

" The perfect man breathes as if he is not breathing " Lao Tze (604 - c.521 BC) Chinese philosopher.

Be observant. If you know people who are healthy, observe for 1-2 minutes how they breathe at rest. What would you see and hear?

What is the pattern of normal breathing?

The duration of inhalations and exhalations, breathing rate, amount of air inhaled per breath, and other parameters are individual. In addition, there are short- and long-term changes. Some healthy people can have the following parameters for the breathing cycle: inhalation (about 2 seconds); exhalation (2-3 seconds); an automatic pause or period of almost no breathing (1 second), the depth of inhalation is about 500–600 ml, and the breathing rate is about 10–12 times per minute.

The picture below shows 4 breathing cycles of normal breathing: inhalation (the upward lines), exhalation (the downward lines), and automatic pause (almost the horizontal lines) accompanied by relaxation of all breathing muscles.

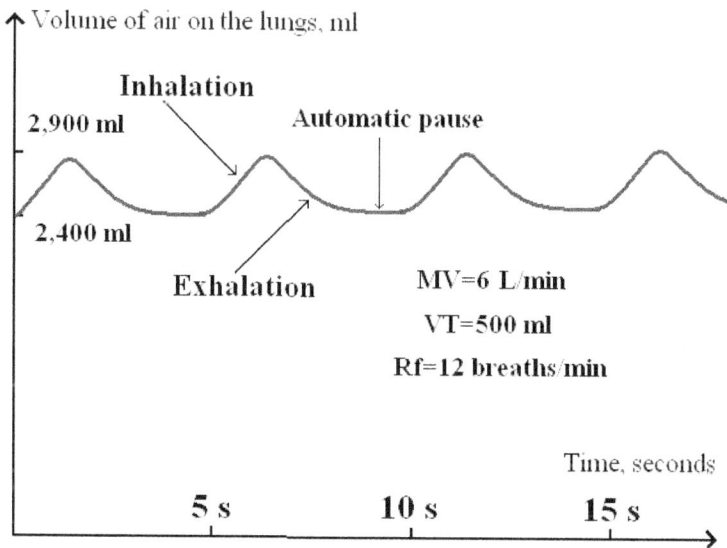

As mentioned above, the person with such breathing is going to have a CP of 40. Up to 80–90% of the inhalation is done by the diaphragm, the main breathing muscle. Exhalation is passive and accompanied by the relaxation of all breathing muscles.

How do sick people usually breathe?
They breathe heavily, with visible (likely chest and belly movements) and audible (possible panting, wheezing, sighing, yawning, sneezing, coughing, deep inhalations, or exhalations) sounds. His mouth may be open. He breathes 12–15 or even more liters of air per minute. He has only 3–5% CO_2 in the lungs and arterial blood. Most cells in his body are CO_2 and O_2 deficient; heavy breathing makes our cells O_2 deficient, as you are going to discover later. His CP is less than 20 seconds.

Be observant. Think about and observe those who are ill. What do you see and hear? What happens with your breathing when you are sick or do not feel well? As mentioned above, the person with such breathing is going to have a CP of 40. Up to 80–90% of the inhalation is done by the diaphragm, the main breathing muscle. Exhalation is passive and accompanied by the relaxation of all breathing muscles.

What is the typical pattern of breathing of sick people? For sick people, the duration of inhalations and exhalations, breathing rate, amount of air inhaled per breath, and other parameters are very individual. Many sick people can have the following parameters of the breathing cycle: inhalation (about 1.5-2 s), exhalation (1.5-2 s), no automatic pause; the depth of inhalation is about 700-1,000 ml; breathing rate is about 15-20 times per minute.

The picture below shows several breathing cycles: inhalation (the upward lines) and exhalation (the downward lines). For sick people the automatic pause between exhalation and inhalation is absent.

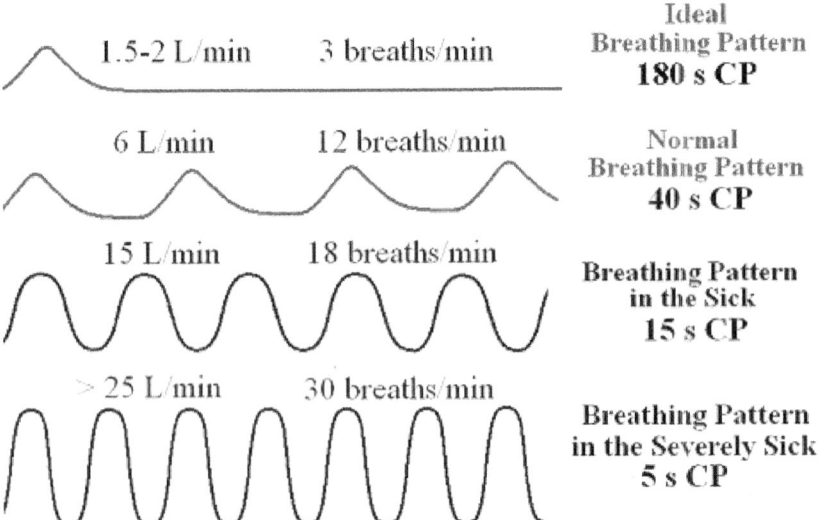

Note that the exhalation of the sick is forceful. Breathing muscles are strained to push air out of the lungs. As was shown above, healthy people just need to relax all their breathing muscles to exhale.

Sometimes sick people have an uneven or irregular breathing pattern that includes sporadic sighing, bouts of coughing, periods of fast breathing, etc. All these patterns reduce body oxygenation. They are symptoms of already existing low oxygenation with a CP of no more than 30.

Measure breath holding time to determine whether you breath normal or fast

You can easily measure whether you breathe normally or fast. As breath-holding time is an accurate and sensitive measure of this, it directly relates to tissue oxygenation. CP stands for control pause, which is the same as breath-holding time.

How can we measure breath-holding time?

Should we measure it after exhalation, after full inhalation, or after 3 or 5 big, deep breaths? While we sit or stand? Should we push the number to its maximum value (hold your breath as much as possible) or stop it at the first signs of air hunger? Out of all these variations, which test is the best representation of oxygenation?

The breath-holding time after a big inhalation is greater than after an exhalation. However, one person may have very strong breathing muscles and a large capacity of the lungs, while another person does not, so this is not a fair measure of breath-holding time because the parameters of the lungs would affect the results in these cases.

What about simple relaxation of the whole body? Such relaxation produces natural, spontaneous exhalation. The end of this natural (not forceful!) exhalation is the best time to start the test.

Is it necessary to pinch the nose? Practice shows that, even with our best intentions, we still breathe through the nose when we try to stop breathing but the nose is not pinched. The air exchange is only 5–15% of usual breathing, but the results would be less accurate. Hence, we need to pinch the nose (and close the mouth!).

Holding a breath for as long as possible is dangerous for many people, for example, due to a dramatic increase in blood pressure. Long breath holds can cause panic attacks or migraine headaches in other people. It makes sense to use a stress-free test, which is performed until the first desire to breathe is felt. Practice shows that this first desire appears together with the involuntary push of the diaphragm or swallowing movement in the throat.

(Your body warns you, "Enough!"). If you stop the test and resume breathing at this moment, you will be able to breathe normally or as before the test. No stress; it is an easy, comfortable test.

Look at the diagram below: after the test, you can breathe as comfortably as before.

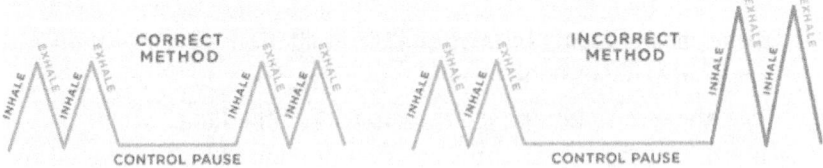

If you hold the breath for too long, the first inhale will be deep and noisy.

Guide to CP

Sit down and rest for 5-7 minutes. Completely relax all your muscles, including the breathing muscles. This relaxation produces natural spontaneous exhalation (breathing out). Pinch your nose at the end of this exhalation and count your CP (breath holding time) in seconds. Keep the nose pinched until you experience the first desire to breathe, so that, after you release the fingers, you can resume your usual breathing (in the same way as you were breathing just before you started to hold your breath). Do not extend your breath holding too far.

You should not gasp for air or open your mouth afterward. The test should be easy and must not cause you stress because it does not interfere with your breathing.

What are the CP norms?

According to the physiological textbook "Essentials of exercise physiology" (McArdle et al, 2000), "If a person breath-holds after a normal exhalation, it takes about 40 seconds before breathing commences".

Russian medical Professor Konstantin Buteyko studied oxygenation, breathing, and this test for decades. During the last four decades, he and his colleagues (over two hundred Russian medical doctors) tested a hundred thousand patients measuring CP many millions of times. These health professionals suggested 60 seconds CP, as a value reflecting, among other things, normal tissue oxygenation and absence of many health problems.

More breathing = less oxygen in tissues

During normal breathing (6 l/min for ventilation and 40 s CP), red blood cells in the lungs become about 98% saturated with oxygen. Breathing more frequently and deeper can slightly increase the oxygenation of our lungs. We can get up to 99% blood saturation with heavier breathing. The increase is small, but what are the effects? And are the effects positive or negative? When one begins to breathe heavily or deeply, the concentrations of CO_2 (carbon dioxide) begin to fall due to an increase in O_2. More CO_2 is removed from the lungs with each breath, and therefore the level of CO_2 in the lungs immediately decreases. In 1-2 minutes, the CO_2 level in the blood falls below its usual levels. In 3-5 minutes most cells of the body (including vital organs and muscles) experience low CO_2 concentrations. In 15–20 minutes, the CO_2 level in the brain is below the norm. Hence, when breathing is heavy all the time, the CO_2 level in all body cells is chronically low. And this is the case with an overwhelming majority of sick people. You might wonder, "But I thought CO_2 was bad." Well, CO_2 and O_2 need to be perfectly balanced, and your breathing controls the balance.

What are the primary physiological effects of low CO_2? CO_2 performs many vital functions in the human body. Here are some of them.

a) CO_2 is one of the key players in the normal oxygenation of cells due to the Bohr effect

The description of this physiological law can be found in standard physiological textbooks since it has been confirmed by dozens of professional studies. What is the Bohr effect? As you know, oxygen is transported in the blood by hemoglobin cells. How do these red cells know where to release more oxygen and where to release less? Or why do they unload more oxygen in areas where it is most needed?

That is because the hemoglobin in the red blood cells is very sensitive to concentrations of CO_2. They make sure the red blood cell releases more O_2 in places with higher concentrations of CO_2. The effect strongly depends on the absolute CO_2 values in the blood and lungs. If the CO_2 concentration is low, O_2 cells stick with the red blood cells because of the presence of hemoglobin. (Scientists call this effect "increased oxygen affinity to hemoglobin." Hence, CO_2 deficiency leads to hypoxia or low oxygenation of the body cells (the suppressed Bohr effect).

The faster and heavier you breathe at rest, the more the Bohr effect is suppressed, and thus oxygenation is low in the cells of our vital organs, like the brain, heart, liver, kidneys, etc.

The Bohr effect is crucial for our survival. At each moment of our lives, some organs and tissues work harder and produce more CO_2. These additional CO_2 concentrations are sensed by the hemoglobin cells, which causes them to release more O_2 in those places where it is most needed. This is a smart self-regulating mechanism for efficient O_2 transport. For example, without the Bohr effect, you could not walk or run for even 3-5 minutes. Because the aerobic system you discovered earlier needs oxygen to be able to perform well. In normal conditions, due to the Bohr effect, more O_2 is released in the muscles that need it, which generates more CO_2. Hence, these muscles, due to an additional oxygen supply, can continue to work at the same high rate.

b) CO_2 is a dilator of blood vessels (arteries and arterioles)

Arteries and arterioles have tiny muscles that can constrict or dilate depending on CO_2 concentrations. At the same time, according to physiological research, the states of these blood vessels are the main factors that define total resistance to blood flow in the body. Normal breathing and normal arterial CO_2 parameters make the resistance to blood flow in the cardiovascular system small, which makes normal blood flow possible. And normal blood flow is important for recovery. Hence, breathing directly participates in the regulation of the heart rate.

When the CO_2 level is low, total resistance increases and vital organs (like the brain, heart, kidneys, liver, stomach, spleen, colon, etc.) get less blood due to the constriction of small blood vessels. This negatively affects the recovery of the body, especially after exercise.

c) CO2 is a natural dilator of bronchi and smaller air passages in the lungs

Normal CO2 concentrations keep these air passages wide open.

When the CO2 level in the lungs is low, the bronchi constrict, causing chest tightness, feelings of breathlessness, suffocation, and wheezing. These effects are particularly important for asthmatics.

d) CO2 gas, when dissolved in the blood, is the second-largest group of negative ions in blood plasma

Hence, breathing directly affects blood pH. In its turn, blood pH is tightly monitored within a very narrow range (from about 7.3 to 7.5) to maintain normal body biochemistry. Therefore, breathing influences concentrations of other ions, including calcium, magnesium, sodium, and potassium, in the blood.

How many people have normal breathing?

If we accept medical standards (6 l/min for ventilation, as in most medical and physiological textbooks, a CP of 40), only a small percentage of the population satisfies this criterion. Experience shows that on average, only a few, if any, per 1,000 people reach the norm of 60 seconds of CP or more.

Most modern people in the West are heavy breathers. They breathe about 8–12 l/min, and their usual CPs are about 20–30 s. For sick people, the parameters are worse. However, more studies are required to find out the exact extent and prevalence of this problem in the general population of different countries and places.

Be observant. You may ask various people to do the breath-holding time test (remember, the test should be easy and comfortable). Do you see the correlation between the way the person breathes and his/her CP? What about the CP of sick and severely sick people? How much is your CP when you feel sick, or have a cold, flu, or infection?

What is a relationship between ventilation and the CP?

The approximate relationship between ventilation and the CP is linear.

If your CP is 30, you breathe twice the norm (about 8 l/min for a 70-kg adult). If your CP is 20 s, you breathe three times the norm (about 12 l/min).

If your CP is 15, you breathe 4 times the norm (about 16 l/min).

If your CP is 10, you breathe 6 times the norm (about 24 l/min).

Often, you may find that the following practical observations are true. If the chest moves with each inhalation-exhalation cycle (at rest while sitting), then the CP is below 30. If, in addition, during breathing, the shoulders move, then the CP is below 20. Finally, if the head moves, the CP is below 10.

Breathing exercises

There are many great breathing exercises, and you will have to determine which one works best for you. To determine the effect of a breathing exercise, you can simply monitor your heart rate. If your heart rate declines, the exercise is effective. I especially like Wim Hof's breathing exercises. I will share my favorite breathing exercise below.

This breathing exercise is simple and easy; everyone can do it! Just follow the steps below. It is recommended to do the exercise right after waking or before a meal when your stomach is still empty. Note that breathing exercises can affect motor control and, in rare cases, lead to loss of consciousness. Therefore, I strongly advise you to sit or lie down before practicing the techniques. Never practice while piloting a vehicle or in or near bodies of water.

- Step 1: Get Comfortable

Assume a meditation posture: sitting, lying down, whichever is most comfortable for you. Make sure you can expand your lungs freely without feeling any constriction.

- Step 2: 30-40 Deep Breaths

Close your eyes and try to clear your mind. Be conscious of your breath, and try to fully connect with it. Inhale deeply through the nose or mouth, and exhale unforcedly through the mouth. Inhale fully through the belly, then the chest, and then exhale naturally. Repeat this 30 to 40 times in short, powerful bursts. You may experience light-headedness and tingling sensations in your fingers and feet. These side effects are completely harmless.

- Step 3: The Hold

After the last exhalation, inhale one final time, as deeply as you can. Then let the air out and stop breathing. Hold until you feel the urge to breathe again.

- Step 4: Recovery Breath

When you feel the urge to breathe again, draw a big breath to fill your lungs and feel your belly and chest expanding. When you are at full capacity, hold your breath for around 15 seconds, then let go. That completes round one. This cycle can be repeated 3–4 times without interruption. After you have completed the breathing exercise, take your time to bask in the bliss. This calm state is highly conducive to meditation; don't hesitate to combine the two.

Breathing while running

As you just discovered, many people breathe faster than necessary. This is also true during exercise, so try to control your breathing. The inhale should take less time than the exhale. You can easily control your breathing by pressing your lips together while exhaling. It's almost as if you're whistling. This will lower your heart rate, which enables you to run at the same pace for longer durations.

Experience story

Arthur (48): "It was only when I started to watch my breathing that I made progress."

Arthur started running at the age of 43. He had always played football (soccer) from childhood until he went to college at eighteen. During his studies, he stopped exercising and slowly gained weight, and his energy level dropped. Arthur has a busy job and three children. One of his children kept him up most nights, making Arthur more stressed. During his vacation, he was still feeling stressed. He realized things had to change. Back from vacation, he decided to go for a run. Just as he always did, he immediately started running three times a week, as fast as possible. After six months, he had more strength in his legs, but his energy level remained low. Shortly after a run, he felt energized and good. But at work, it seemed as if he was getting more tired. Once, he attended a lecture on breathing and running. It was there that Arthur first heard about the connection between rapid breathing and fatigue. Since that lecture, Arthur has been practicing breathing exercises directly after waking up and controlling his breathing during his runs. He has also started to go for less intense runs, and now he notices that he is regaining energy. "It's funny that by running less far and less fast, I get a lot more effect from my training," notes Arthur. Can you relate this story to the supercompensation model discussed in Chapter 1, and find the flaws in his previous exercise plan of running three times a week at maximum effort?

I hope that after reading this chapter, you will try the breathing exercises yourself. I also advise you to monitor your progress by measuring your CP.

Breathing exercises that enable you to recover well, in combination with varied training, are a powerful combination, with which you will certainly make progress and regain energy. In the next chapter, I explain how you can apply the correct training load to make sure your performance increases.

Chapter 3: Training load

Heart rate

Running based on heart rate is one of the best ways to control the training load of your training. The workouts are catered to your specific needs and will certainly help you run faster than ever before. For each heart rate zone, I have written down a feeling when running in that specific zone. Zones 1, 2, and 3 are aerobic activities. Zones 4 and 5 are anaerobic.

- Zone 1: slow breathing, comfortable able to talk, and breathing can be delayed
- Zone 2: slow breathing, able to talk, breathing can be slightly delayed
- Zone 3: breathing is faster than usual, still able to talk, although long sentences will need another breath
- Zone 4: breathing fast, unable to talk
- Zone 5: breathing very fast, muscles building lactate acid

Determine lactate threshold heart rate

All training schedules in this book will use the heart rate zones mentioned above. To determine your heart rate zones you will need to determine your lactate threshold. You can determine your lactate threshold in 2 ways. You can buy an exercise test from a therapist, and they will professionally measure your VO2 max, lactate threshold, and maximum heart rate. Most exercise tests cost approximately 200 dollars.

If you don't want to spend as much on an exercise test, but do want to determine your lactate threshold you can either run 1 hour as fast as possible or perform the Conconi test.

1 hour run

If you run 1 hour as fast as possible, your average heart rate during this event is your lactate threshold. But this is only accurate if you go as fast as you can, you can probably tell yourself, but in general, this means that you're no longer able to go even slightly faster towards the end because you're so tired. And around the halfway mark you begin wondering whether you'll be able to go on at the current pace. A 10k or 15k race is usually a great way to perform this test.

Conconi test

The Conconi test is famous for its simplicity and accuracy.

1. Run 6 minutes as a warming up at an average pace of 7 km/h (4.35 mi/h)
2. Next every 2 minutes the average pace will increase by 1 km/h. After the 6-minute warming up you will run 2 minutes at a pace of 8 km/h (4.97 mi/h), then 2 minutes at 9 km/h (5.59 mi/h), and so on.
3. You keep on going until you're completely exhausted. This is a test in which you will have to go all out. So be prepared and make sure you do everything you can.
4. If your legs are exploding and you can't run anymore, you will need to check your heart rate. Some watches will remember the maximum heart rate, but one can never be too sure.
5. Your lactate threshold can be determined quite simply, based on your maximum heart rate and your maximum pace during the test.

Attention: the maximum heart rate achieved during this test is not your maximum heart rate.

A speed of 20 km/h (12.42 mph or higher)?

Your lactate threshold is 6 beats lower than the maximum heart rate during the test.

A speed of 18-19 km/h (11.18-11.80 mph)?

Your lactate threshold is 5 beats lower than the maximum heart rate during the test.

A speed of 16-17 km/h (9.94-10.56 mph)?

Your lactate threshold is 4 beats lower than the maximum heart rate during the test.

A speed of 14-15 km/h (8.69-9.32 mph)?

Your lactate threshold is 3 beats lower than the maximum heart rate during the test.

A speed of 12-13 km/h (7.45-8.07 mph)?

Your lactate threshold is 2 beats lower than the maximum heart rate during the test.

A speed of 10-11 km/h (6.21-6.83 mph)?

Your lactate threshold is 1 beat lower than the maximum heart rate during the test.

I recommend doing this test with someone either running or cycling beside you so that they can focus on the correct pace, and you only have to focus on giving it your all.

Now to determine your heart rate zones you simply multiply your lactate threshold heart rate with the appropriate factor. As I did in the table below.

Heart rate zone	Multiplier	Lactate threshold Heart rate	From	To
Z1	0,675	188	127	136
Z2	0,725	188	136	150
Z3	0,8	188	150	169
Z4	0,9	188	169	183
Z5	0,975	188	183	193
AI	1,025	188	193	202

Although 200 dollars is expensive, I advise you to buy an exercise test. It is more important to know your lactate threshold heartbeat exactly than to have the best heart rate monitor available. I would rather train with a cheap heart rate monitor of 50 dollars that has an error of 2 heartbeats while knowing my lactate threshold accurately. Then an expensive watch that has no error, but running 10 heartbeats too high or low because my lactate threshold heart rate is not accurately determined.

Running mileage
When you see how much is written about running injuries, you would think injuries are a fact of life for runners you have to learn to live with them. This is nonsense, of course. Of course, you can run injury-free. But what causes many injuries?

Maarten Fornerod wrote an interesting article about the causes of injuries. "There has been a lot of research into running injuries, and each time two factors are important: training volume and previous injuries. The more you run, the higher the risk of injury. That seems obvious, but there is one important detail: it is not the intensity with which you run but it is the distance associated with injuries."

What causes most running injuries?

When you start running five tissues receive an extra load on them: muscles, tendons, bones, cartilage, and ligaments. Ligaments? Ligaments connect two bones, and tendons connect a muscle and a bone. Just look at it the next time you eat a chicken leg.

The muscles, bones, and ligaments adapt quickly to a new training load. They are used to the new load in ten to twenty weeks. However, this does not apply to the tendons and the cartilage. They take much longer to adapt. At least two years! That means that if your muscles, bones, and ligaments are already well adapted to the extra training load, your cartilage and tendons are far from adapted see the figure below.

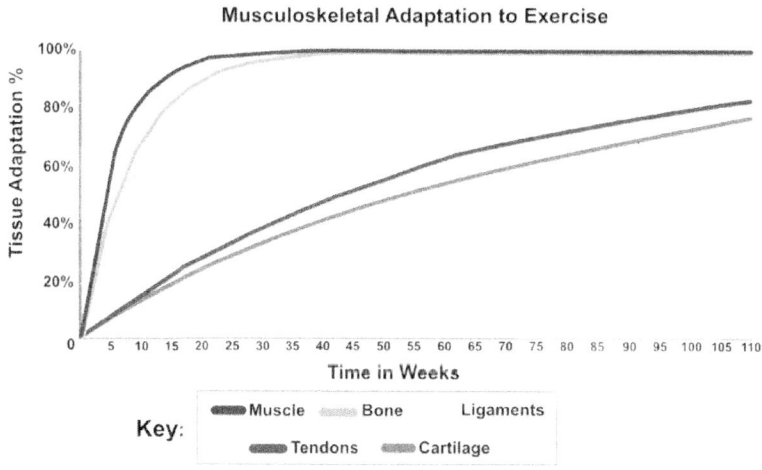

Tissue adaptation at new load. Schematic image of the adaptation of different tissues by load

Most novice runners or novice marathon runners are increasing the load on the cartilage and tendons too fast. The muscles, heart, and lungs can handle the new training load, but the cartilage and tendons can't. They get overloaded, which leads to injuries, most often with the knees, shin splints, Achilles, ankle, and sole. Once you have an injury it will probably nag you for quite a long time. Why? Just look at the graph: it may take another year to a year and a half for the knee or Achilles tendons to adjust, so don't expect to get rid of it after a month of rest. A year much slower. At least.

It is, therefore, best to avoid this overload of cartilage and tendon when increasing the training load, such as when training for a marathon.

The solution to avoiding these injuries is quite simple. As Fornerod suggests the training distance per week is related to those injuries. And research also suggests that a correct running form can prevent injuries. The distance is controlled by following the suggested training schedules. Moreover, I describe the easiest way to improve your running form.

Running form
Overloading the cartilage and tendons is not only related to running mileage but also running technique. Although a correct running form is complex, one variable can drastically prevent injuries.

Arm carriage and correct footfall are important for developing an efficient running form, but the easiest way to improve your form and reduce the load on your body is to focus on running cadence. The perfect cadence can vary by individual. But a cadence of 170 and higher is ideal. A higher cadence decreases the vertical loading rate and the stress on the skeletal system. In particular, it decreases the vertical loading rate of the knees, hips, and lower back. Moreover, running cadence is linked to running economy because it affects the way you strike the ground. Better form and optimal cadence translate into an improved running economy and faster times.

Retraining running cadence
Retraining cadence is easy to learn for 90 percent of people. While it is next to impossible to adequately judge your form while you're running, counting your strides for one minute is simple. Start your watch and begin counting. Many recreational runners run with a cadence between 150 and 155 times per minute.

Improving your cadence is easiest when you concentrate on your arm carriage. For most people, the cadence is dependent upon how fast they can move their arms while running. Most professionals have a very short arm carriage, as they have a short angle at the elbow. This affects the position of the hand when the arm is carried forward. Most elite long-distance runners have an arm swing, that ends with their hands near their hearts. Some elite women even have an even shorter angle at the elbow, resulting in an arm swing with their hands near the collar bone. The main benefits of a higher arm swing are that it requires less energy to perform and that it takes less time to travel the arm back and forth. Your new arm carriage allows you to move your arms faster, allowing you to run with a higher cadence. In turn, this will decrease the load on your body, while also making you a more efficient runner. If you are interested in seeing some footage, I advise you to look at Eliud Kipchoge.

A metronome can also be a great tool to increase your cadence, most smartwatches have this functionality. There are plenty of places you can download a metronome set to 170 beats per minute. Alternatively, download 10 to 15 songs that are around 170 beats per minute. Check online for recommendations or download a program that analyzes songs and lists the beats per minute. You can even drag in slower songs and have them reset to 170 bpm.

The transition to a faster cadence may feel foreign. But as you achieve that desired rhythm, it will become second nature. Soon you'll find yourself running faster and more efficiently, getting you a little closer to the pros.

Experiences

Many runners train a lot in Zone 4, often close to or even above the anaerobic threshold (more on that later). This is a shame because you can build up too much fatigue if your recovery is not optimal. That is why I encourage runners to run in Zone 2 and especially Zone 3.

The zone 2 and zone 3 workouts are ideally suited to get your energy efficiency in order. As I mentioned earlier in this chapter, you have enough energy-efficient fats to last for hours, but your carbohydrate supply is limited and will only last for a short time. In Zone 2 and Zone 3, you learn to run faster on these frugal fats. So, you use less energy, but you can achieve higher average speeds. So, double the benefit. Also, these are the zones that enable you to lose weight, if necessary.

In the beginning, zone 3 workouts will, for some runners, feel like a regression. The pace might be slower, and the training does not always feel satisfying and can feel boring. If a zone 3 workout doesn't feel good at first, take a closer look at your breathing. Rapid breathing (due to stress) makes running at a slow pace feel uncomfortable. By deliberately extending your exhalation, you will be able to lower your heart rate, this allows you to run faster. With a heart rate monitor, you can easily measure whether these workouts are working. If you run faster at the same heart rate, then you are making great progress. The story of Steve and Ivy is a good example.

Steve and Ivy are both in their mid-twenties. They were inspired to start running by reading about a woman with chronic fatigue, who ran a marathon. The story touched them because Ivy herself suffered from chronic fatigue. To Steve, running was not new, as he had been running intensively for a few years and regularly participated in a 10-kilometer competition. Ivy, however, did not have any running experience. Before she started training, Ivy did an exercise test, and her heart rate zones were determined. Ivy's training pace was significantly slower than Steve's regular pace, but Steve always ran next to her, partly out of love and partly out of concern. To his surprise, Steve saw that his performance on the 10 kilometers had improved considerably. "But I train more slowly than ever," he said in amazement.

Steve discovered by chance that he ran in a too-high heart rate zone, and by training in the aerobic zones, his performance improved considerably.

Chapter 4: Exercises to remain injury free

The distance you run and cadence can prevent common injuries. But it is always advisable to build your injury resistance. In this chapter, you will discover exercises that prevent the most common running injuries. Some will even improve your running economy, which will lead to faster race times. I always advise you to perform the exercises at a pain-free level and progress the exercise over time. I recommend you to do the workouts twice a week. A workout takes less than 15 minutes, and to save time you can perform them in your regular clothes because you probably won't break a sweat performing them.

Preventing knee, calf and achilles injuries

ATG split squat

The ATG Split Squat checks a lot of boxes when it comes to improving strength and mobility. Let's work our way up the kinetic chain to explain why this exercise is so valuable.

1. Ankles: If we follow a joint by joint approach, we want the ankle to be mobile and the knee to be stable. If the former isn't the case, then the latter won't be either. With the ATG split squat, athletes are loading ankle dorsiflexion through their largest possible range of motion. This more so than stretching is the most effective way to make lasting mobility adaptations.
2. Knee: In the simplest form, training is designed to prepare your tissues for the demand of your sport and activity. Developing structural strength is important as it's a position seen during high-velocity change of direction and jumping takeoff. The function of the Quadriceps is to stabilize the patella and extend the knee. The ATG Split Squat is very effective for strengthening this muscle group. While we're unable to correlate specific metrics in the gym to injury

prevention, this could have implications for protecting the ligaments in the knee.
3. Hip Flexors: "Tight" hips typically need to be strengthened not stretched (while also looking at Pelvic position). With muscles being weakest at their end ranges of motion, we know that "tightness" can be a protective mechanism for the Nervous System to avoid muscles being overly lengthened. During the ATG Split Squat, we see the Hip Flexor of the trail leg strengthened through a full range of motion. This signals the body to be more confident in accessing a greater range of motion.

The movement can be regressed and progressed according to your current movement capacity and strength level.

To do the exercise:

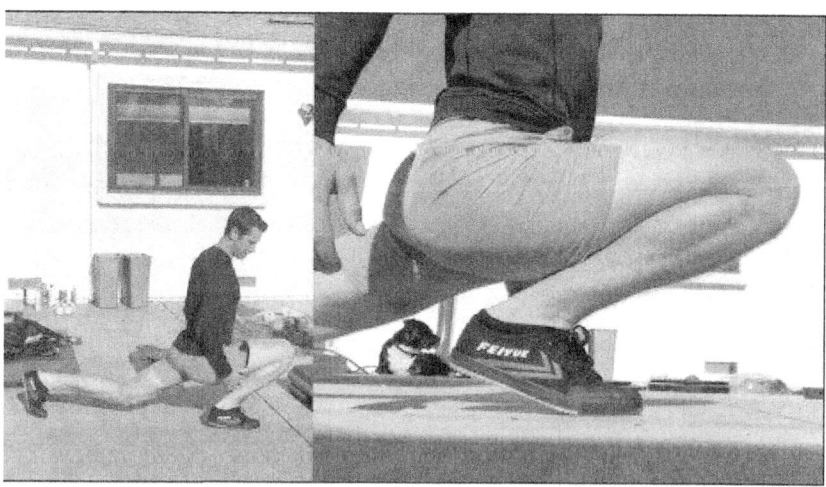

1. Start by standing up tall.
2. Step forward with one foot. Make sure you have a wide stance.
3. Drive the front knee down and forward. Until you reach a position in which the back muscles of your leg press

against the calf. Your rear knee should not touch the ground. Depending upon your Achilles flexibility you can lift your heel off the ground. The photo above is a good illustration of the perfect ATG split squat form.
   4. Press your front leg up to return to the starting position.

You can adjust the ATG split squat to your current level. If you increase the elevation of the front foot the exercise will be easier. And if you decrease the elevation of the front foot the exercise will be more difficult. Furthermore, depending on the flexibility of your Achilles, you can elevate your heel. Performing the exercise with your front foot flat on the ground is more difficult and requires more flexibility of your Achilles.

It is a hard exercise to perform, so start easy. Always make sure you have perfect form, as this will benefit your mobility and strength the most. What matters is that you start doing this exercise. As an example, I started on two steps of the stairs with my heel elevated, before slowly decreasing the elevation. Recently I have just performed my first flat foot ATG split squat.

Moreover, it is possible to perform this exercise with added weight to increase your strength even more. But remember that form is crucial. I would advise you to be careful about adding weights. Only start adding weights when you can comfortably perform 10 ATG split squats on an even surface with your front foot flat.

Peterson step up

To do the exercise:

1. Start by placing the exercising leg on the step, with the resting leg on the floor.
2. The heel of the resting leg will be slightly ahead of the toe of your working leg.
3. The working leg (on the step) will be slightly bent, heel raised, with your weight on the ball of your foot.
4. Slowly push through the ball of your exercising leg and let your heel touch the step.
5. Your resting leg will remain ahead of the toe on the exercising leg.

Why do these exercises positively impact the Achilles?

A tendon is what connects your muscle to your bone. As you discovered earlier the adaptation of the tendons is slow, however, our muscles adapt much faster and can protect your tendons and ligaments. The Achilles is the largest and strongest tendon in your body and much force is exerted on the Achilles tendon while running. The muscles that can protect the Achilles tendons are located in the calf. You have two different calf muscles, and the lower, deeper one: the soleus, is the one that relates most to protecting your Achilles. The soleus also has the strongest pull of any muscle in your body. Your soleus naturally gets trained when your knees go over your toes, so performing these exercises will strengthen your achilles tendon, as will calf raises because calf raises train both the calf muscles.

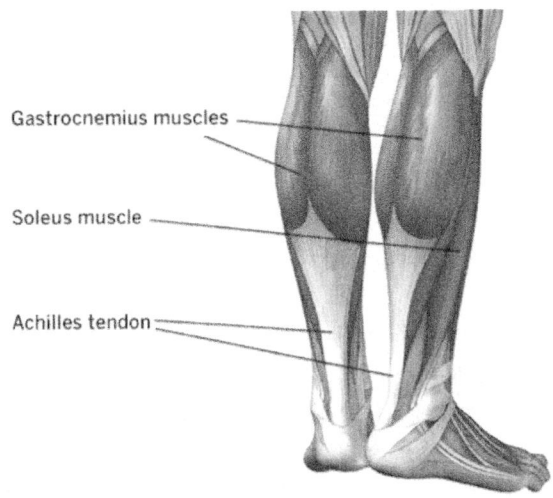

Nordic hamstring curl

According to a recent study including the Nordic hamstring exercise in injury prevention programs halves the rate of hamstring injuries.

To do the exercise:

1. Start in a tall kneeling position with your hips extended and feet secured.
2. You will want to have some kind of pad to kneel on to make it more comfortable for your knees. A yoga mat can be a good option. Alternatively, you could use a towel, pillow, or blanket.
3. To secure your ankles/calves, you can have someone hold them down, fit them under something, or rig up some other option. I perform them under the first step of the stairs. Be careful not to secure your heels, as the force applied upon the place you secure yourself with is applying much force.

4. Once set up, you can then start to fall forwards slowly. As you fall forwards, you want to fight to maintain your hip extension angle and not flex as you come to the ground. You also want to fight to resist your knee extending, using your hamstrings as much as possible. This combination will force your hamstrings to work and maximize the benefit of the exercise.
5. After your reach the ground and get to full knee extension, you can either curl back up or push up back up with the use of your arms.

The movement automatically scales to your current movement capacity and strength level, as this influences how far you can fight the force of your body falling forward.

Reverse Nordic

This is a simple movement, but maintaining strict positioning is vital to get the full benefits. Here's how to do it:

1. Grab a mat, or make sure you're on a soft floor. Kneel, and sit on top of your feet

2. If trying this exercise for the first time, place the knees and feet close together, approximately hip-width apart. If you are more advanced, have the feet and knees slightly wider, just outside the hips, so you can lay back farther without hitting your legs.
3. Sit up in a tall kneeling position, push the hips forward, and lock the rib cage down. You're looking to create a straight line down the front of your body, especially at the hips. This is to create a stretch of the hip flexor muscles.
4. Lower the shoulders towards the floor by bending the knee, while maintaining the "plank" position created. If hip extension is maintained, and the core adequately braced, there should be no strain on the low back, and you will feel an intense stretch down the front of the legs.
5. Continue to lean back as far as it is possible to control, then squeeze the quads to return to the starting position (this may not be very far, to begin with). It is crucial to not let the hips drop backward at any point during the movement. If they do, the stretch on the hip flexors will be released, defeating the point of the exercise.

VMO squat

You perform this exercise like a regular squat. The difference is that your heels are elevated quite high at about a 45-degree angle. This enables you to lower into full knee flexion while keeping a perfectly upright torso, which isolates the quadriceps, especially the VMO.

To do the exercise:

1. Elevate your heels to a 45-degree angle. I perform this exercise on an elevated doorstep, but you can also buy a slant board.
2. Place your feet shoulder with apart.
3. Slowly bend your knees while keeping your torso erect. Do not lean forward. At the bottom of your movement, your hamstrings will cover your calves. Maintain constant, slow, and controlled muscle tension.

4. Return to starting position while keeping your torso and back erect. Exhale as you push through your heels and stand tall.

Preventing shin, calf and Achilles injuries

Tibialis raises

The shinbone, or tibia, absorbs a lot of shock from impact during running. As a result, it's particularly prone to injuries, both mundane and serious.

A recent scientific review by Maarten Moen and colleagues at a medical center in the Netherlands concluded that shin splints, viewed as an irritating but ordinary problem, and tibial stress fractures, a serious bone injury, are caused by the same phenomenon: bending of the tibia during running.

Now, the tibia doesn't bend like a wet noodle; it's more like a bridge under strain. After your foot hits the ground during running, the force traveling up your legs puts stress on your shin, causing it to bend slightly backward. The degree to which your shinbone bends depends on two factors. How thick the bone is, and how well the bone is supported by the muscles surrounding it. Fortunately, having strong calf muscles and tibialis muscles helps on both of these fronts.

Getting back to our bridge analogy, the calf muscles are like the strong cables on a suspension bridge. When the muscles tense up, as they do during impact with the ground, they counter the bending forces that are attempting to deform and strain the tibia. So, in theory, runners with stronger calf muscles will be more resistant to a shin injury.

This hypothesis was put to the test in a 2007 study by Luke Madeley, Shannon Munteanu, and Daniel Bonanno at la Trobe University in Australia. Like Popp's study, Madeley and his two fellow researchers compared two groups of runners: one with shin splints, and one without. Both groups were asked to complete as many consecutive single-leg calf raises as possible, with the researchers ensuring they didn't "cheat" by going too low or leaning forward.

As predicted, the injured runners averaged only 23 calf raises, with the healthy runners averaging 33, a difference of 30%!

Band Tibialis raise

To start strengthening your tibialis anterior muscle to correct your foot drop, obtain an elastic resistance band. You can get one from your physical therapist, or you can buy one at your local sporting goods store.

Secure your band to a stable object for instance behind the door or tied to a pole. Tie a loop in your band and secure it around your foot near your toes. It may be helpful to have your lower leg resting on a small pillow so the heel of your foot does not rub on the ground.

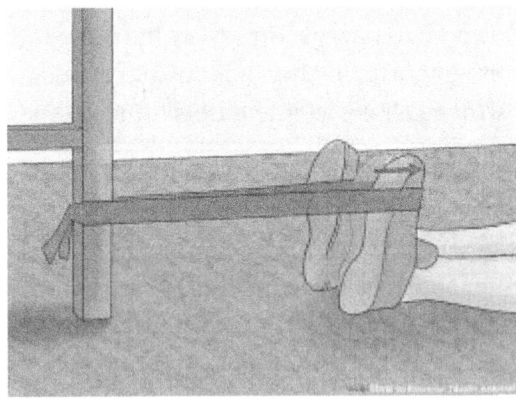

To do the exercise:

1) Pull your toes and foot up while keeping your knee straight. Only your ankle should move as you flex your foot up

2) Pull your foot up as far as you can, hold the end position for a second or two.
3) Slowly relax back to the starting position.
4) Repeat.

Standing Tibialis raise

Another great exercise for your tibialis muscles is the standing tibialis raise.

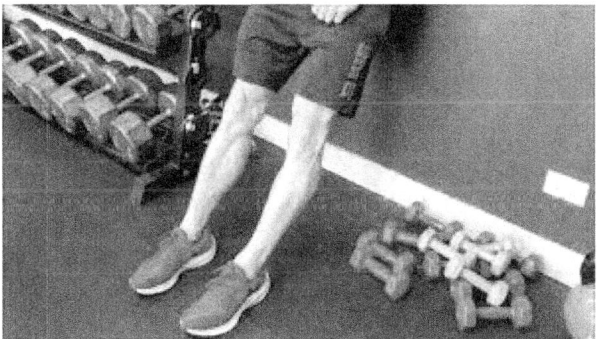

Another great exercise for your tibialis muscles is the standing tibialis raise.

To do the exercise:

1. Stand with your back against a wall. Just like the picture above. Move your feet slightly in front of the wall. Then press your back against the wall and lift your toes, while keeping your knee straight (don't overextend the knee). Only your toes should move upwards. The further your feet are from the wall the harder the exercise is.
2. Pull your foot up as far as you can, hold the end position for a second or two.
3. Then slowly lower your toes, so that your foot will again be fully connected with the ground.
4. Repeat.

You can make this exercise harder by placing your feet further from the wall, or you could eventually perform it one leg at a time.

Calf raises

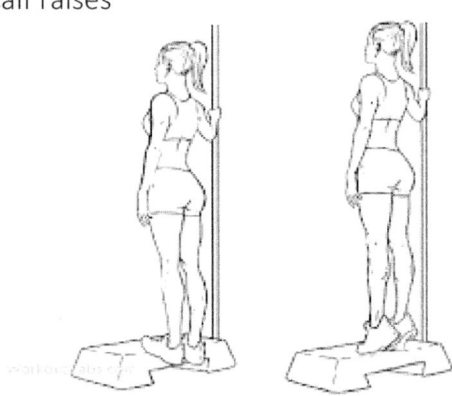

To do the exercise:

1) Stand up straight, then push through the balls of your feet and raise your heel until you are standing on your toes.
2) Then lower slowly back to the start.
3) repeat

Calf raises are just about the easiest exercise to slip into your day-to-day life. Do them while brushing your teeth, or waiting for the kettle to boil. You can make the exercise harder by elevating your feet on a step of the stairs. Allowing your heels to drop more and increasing the range of motion. Or you could perform the exercise on one leg or you can increase the weights by performing the exercise with dumbbells.

Hip stretchers

Picture a strong runner racing toward the finish line of a race. The arms are pumping front to back, the knees are driving and the runner is probably leaning slightly into his stride as he fires off the ground with each step. At first glance, his power and forward progression look to be coming from the force with which he pushes off the ground. The foot strikes the ground, his calves flex and he fires up and forward.

If you were to look at that runner in slow motion, however, you may notice that the real power comes from farther up the kinetic chain at the hamstrings, hips, and glutes. Those are the muscles that are essential for running strength and efficiency. This may come as no surprise when you consider the fact that the gluteus medius, minimus, and maximus make up the largest muscle group in the body. Those, along with the surrounding hip and hamstring muscles, make for a real powerhouse when it comes to running. It thus makes sense to train these muscles.

1. Place the band around your laces, then begin moving one knee upwards, until your thigh is parallel with the floor.
2. Hold this position for 1-3 seconds and then slowly place your foot back on the ground.
3. Repeat (both legs)

You can make this exercise harder by using stiffer bands or you can hold the position with your thigh parallel to the floor longer.

Glutes

To do the exercise:

1. Lie on the ground on your back and bend your knees at 90 degrees.
2. Lift your hips off the floor by pushing your heels to the ground.
3. Lift your hips high, so they are in one line with your knees and the shoulders.
4. At the top, focus on squeezing your glutes together.
5. Now lower the hips, and lift them again.

You can make this exercise harder by performing it with one leg. Starting with one leg up in the sky with a bend, eventually working your way up to stretching the leg parallel to the bridge your body forms.

Proposed workouts

I advise you to perform two workouts a week. It will roughly take you 10 to 15 minutes to complete the workout. And you probably won't break a sweat. I like to perform one exercise directly after another, allowing me to squeeze a workout into a busy day. I like to mix it up a little. Once a week I perform workout A, and another day I follow workout B

Workout A
Two times:

1. Calf raise 10x

2. ATG split squad 10x
3. Hip flexor 10x
4. Peterson step 10x up
5. Nordic curl 10x
6. Reverse Nordic 10x
7. Band tibialis raise 10x
8. Glute bridge 10x

Workout B
Two times:

1. Calf raise 10x
2. ATG split squad 10x
3. Hip flexor 10x
4. VMO squat 10x
5. Nordic curl 10x
6. Reverse Nordic 10x
7. Standing tibialis raise 10x
8. Glute bridge 10x

Chapter 5: Theory of the training schedules

I am a big fan of the marathon, not because of the stories surrounding it but because the body is so perfectly balanced at the marathon heart rate. Earlier, I wrote about possible health gains from running, and training for a marathon is the ultimate medicine.

A quick reminder: You only have about one to two hours' worth of fast carbohydrates in your blood, muscles, and liver, and you have fats for weeks. For people with burnout or other stress-related issues, the number of carbohydrates is even lower, because they burn carbohydrates at rest. Their minds are rushed, and their breathing is too fast. By doing breathing exercises and running, you can partly solve this (or practice another sport). Running at your marathon heart rate is likely a great match. A nice side effect is that fat burning is stimulated, and after some time, carbohydrate burning decreases. Moreover, fitness improves. As a result, I advise runners to run as much as they can at their marathon heart rate, using their frugal fats as fuel.

If you run 5 kilometers (3.10 miles) as fast as possible, you are constantly running above your anaerobic threshold. Great for fit athletes who find it important to run those 5 kilometers (3.10 miles) as fast as possible, but useless for people who primarily exercise to feel better in addition to exercising. And a total disaster for those suffering from diabetes, obesity, or burnout. For many runners, the marathon heart rate is high in zone 2 or low in zone 3.

You can never burn 100% fat in real life, and you can never burn 100% carbohydrates. You always burn both energy supplies. But as you increase your heart rate, you will burn more and more carbohydrates and fewer and fewer fats.

Look at the table below, zone 3 is the heart rate at which the burning of both energy stores is in balance, although the specific heartbeat varies for each individual. Anyone who runs a marathon between 3:30 and 4:00 will run a marathon in heart rate zone 3. Perfect for lifestyle diseases where the energy systems don't function properly.

Heart rate zone	Energy system	Fuel
Zone 1	100% aerobic	Fat
Zone 2	75% aerobic 25% anaerobic	75% fat 25% carbohydrates
Zone 3	50% aerobic 50% anaerobic	50% fat 50% carbohydrates
Zone 4	25% aerobic 75% anaerobic	25% fat 75% carbohydrates
Zone 5	100% anaerobic	100% carbohydrates

People with fatigue complaints continuously use their energy-fast sugars as fuel. A problem with diabetes, obesity, or fatigue, among other things. However, incorrect energy storage burning is not irreversible. Eating well, resting well, and correctly exercising can ensure that you use your frugal fats as fuel again. And you do train correctly by running at marathon heart rate (or cycling in the beginning).

Is a marathon too much for you? That is fine. Then train for a marathon, without running it. But I hope to give you a push to run a marathon. In a responsible way.

Can you run a marathon with a maximum training distance of 14 kilometers (8.69 miles)?

Yes.

Thousands have already done so. Before I explain the training schedule, I first explain how this schedule was developed. I also look at the current schedules, where you often train longer than 30 kilometers (18.64 miles) in the run-up to your marathon.

There are two key points you need to know to complete the 14-kilometer (8.69 miles) plan:

1. How do you build up the four training sessions per week?
2. What's your marathon heart rate?

In this part of the book, I describe how you can accurately determine your marathon heart rate and how you can build up your training.

Training based on heart rate

Scientists have discovered that you can accurately predict at what heart rate someone can run a marathon.

Just repeat.

What scientists discovered was that you can accurately predict at what heart rate someone can run a marathon.

And if you know at what heart rate someone can run a marathon, it makes sense to train your body to adapt to running at that specific heart rate.

You already know how to determine your anaerobic threshold and your heart rate zones. Science has already discovered how long you can run in each specific heart rate zone. So your marathon heart rate is determined by your anaerobic threshold and how long it will take you to run a marathon. Below, you see the different heart rate zones and how long you can keep it up with that heart rate, provided you have trained (very) well.

Heart rate zone	Time your able to run
< ZONE 1	8 hours
ZONE 1	6 hours

ZONE 2	4 hours
ZONE 3	3 hours
Anaerobic threshold heart rate	2 hours
Above Anaerobic threshold (low in zone 5)	15 minutes
Far above Anaerobic threshold (high in zone 5)	60 seconds
All out	10 seconds

Marathon runners, therefore, have different marathon heart rates depending on their finish times. Some runners run a marathon in zone 1 because it takes them six hours to complete a marathon. However, if Mo Farah is going to run for six hours, he will not run a marathon, but 100 kilometers (62.13 miles).

Another example is; do you run a marathon in four hours? Then heart rate zone 2 is a good heart rate zone to run the marathon, as you can see in the table above. However, for an experienced runner like Iwan Kamminga, this zone is too low, he can safely run a marathon in zone 3 because he runs 60 kilometers (37.28 miles) in 3:59:29.

So, if you know what your body is capable of doing at the moment during a marathon, you can train very specifically, and you will be well prepared and recover faster.

It's a complex matter, but after reading this part, all you have to do is choose a great marathon, predict your finish time, train on your marathon heart rate, and incorporate some speedwork.

Interval training

During your training week, you will always work on your speed. Most recreational runners tend to do a lot of long runs at a slow pace. But if you think about this, the whole approach couldn't be further from the reality of running in a race. You are training to run slowly, as you can tell by your running form. The average cadence is likely around 155 steps per minute. This also makes you more prone to injuries, as you discovered earlier. In a race, you will need to run a lot faster and with a higher cadence, which makes the race pace feel horrible. Moreover, your form also makes you more prone to injuries, as you discovered earlier.

In the training schedule described in this book, however, you will run shorter distances. This allows you to run faster, with better form, making you more efficient. Speed training is also incorporated to make your body adapt to higher speeds. The basic theory is that your finish time depends on how fast you can run. If your fastest pace is 5 minutes per kilometer (8.03 minutes per mile) and you want to be able to run a marathon within 3.30 hours, then it will feel as if you're sprinting the whole marathon. Your heart rate will be higher because you have trouble controlling your breathing. If, however, you can run 1 kilometer in 3 minutes (4.50 minutes per mile),

running at 4 minutes per kilometer (6.26 per mile) will feel comfortable, and you can easily control your breath. Allowing you to lower your heart rate. Moreover, your running form will become efficient, allowing you to conserve more energy with every stride.

As opposed to most interval methods described by other coaches you will perform the intervals below your anaerobic threshold. This is a fast but easy pace. Moreover, you will have time to recover after each interval. Remember the goal is to become faster, which is only possible if you can start your next interval relatively fresh. You probably have done an interval workout in which your pace dropped considerably after each completed interval. When you train like this, you're no longer training your running economy, which is what you need to do if you want to run faster.

Why do other runners do very long runs

I have looked at several popular training schedules for the marathon, and many of them are similar to the schedule on RunnersWeb.com.

The RunnersWeb schedule starts with six training days, and the longest run is 16 kilometers (9.94 miles). There is also an hour of cross-training in between. Immediately in week 1, you train five times and run 42 kilometers (26 miles), and you do another sport for an hour! That is already more than you would do with the Run By Heart Rates marathon training schedule in the toughest week. In Run by Heart Rate's toughest week, you will run four times: twice, 14 kilometers (9 miles); once, a speed workout of 9 kilometers (5 miles); and once, a recovery run of 7 kilometers (4 miles), totaling 44 kilometers (27 miles). Compare this to RunnersWeb's toughest week, and the difference in mileage is huge: 76 kilometers (47.22 miles) compared to Run by Heart Rate's toughest week with 44 kilometers (27 miles).

What is particularly striking about the regular training plans is that long-distance endurance training is regularly followed by even longer-distance training immediately the following week. For example, in week 10, you train 70 kilometers (43.49 miles) in total, and the longest distance you train is 30 kilometers (18.64 miles). A week later, you train 76 kilometers (47.22 miles) in total, and the longest training is 32 kilometers (19.88 miles).

It scared me just by reading it. I would not think about running 30 kilometers (18.64 miles) on Sunday and then training for 76 kilometers (47.22 miles) again the following week, including an endurance run of 32 kilometers. When does the body have time to recover? Never!! This will also put you at high risk for developing injuries, and most likely you will not even finish the training plan. This excessive mileage occurs not only with marathon training plans but also with beginner training plans for people who want to run their first 5K or 10K race.

Imagine the daily lives of people following regular schedules. Their days must revolve around running, making it no longer fun. By following the schedules in this book, running doesn't have to interfere with your everyday life. If you want to run a marathon, your maximum training distance will be 14 kilometers (8.69 miles). So you can spend the rest of your time doing the things you love while still achieving all the goals you're after and improving your personal best times!

The benefit of these "old" running schedules, however, is that they have a proven track record. There have been hundreds of thousands of runners who have run marathons with this kind of schedule. So you know it works. But where do these schedules originate?

Training schedules with so much mileage date back a long time. Elite runners have run great times with these schedules. Since the 1960s, the marathon world record has been broken from 2:08:34 (by Australian Derek Clayton) to 2:02:57 (by Kenyan Dennis Kimetto).

Making a lot of kilometers works well. Why else would you do it?

As opposed to the 1960s, 1970s, and 1980s, a new group of marathon runners has emerged—a group of runners that runs much slower. To show the number of "slow" runners (by this I mean runners who take longer than three hours to complete the marathon; that's quite fast, but it wasn't in the past), we have the participants of the Berlin Marathon from 1985 and 2014 side by side.

	1985 Berlin	2014 Berlin
Participants	9810	28.946
Runners finished within 3 hours	1758	1261
Runners finished within 4 hours	7975	13996
Slowest runner	5:23;52	7:18:01

These are interesting numbers. In 2014, 19,136 more people will participate in the marathon. But fewer people finish within three hours, not just relatively but also in an absolute sense. That is significant. In 1985, more than eighty percent of the participants finished within four hours. In 2014, however, less than half of the participants finished within four hours. In short, nowadays more people run marathons, but they run slower.

Someone who runs the marathon within 2:30 will complete his 30-kilometer (18.64 miles) endurance training within two hours, while someone who runs the marathon within 4 or 4:30 completes his 30-kilometer (18.64 miles) training in 3:30 hours. So the training is much longer and thus more intense for the amateur runner, which also makes the need for recovery bigger. This raises the question of whether training like a professional athlete in terms of mileage is advisable. Of course, I can't tell how well runners recover. However, I do know that the recovery of amateur runners is probably worse than the recovery of professional athletes because you are less fit and will probably need to work during the day. You might wonder, isn't it just better not to run a marathon?

Most certainly not. What matters most is that you find a balance between training load and recovery, making it possible to achieve the benefits of supercompensation. Moreover, if you run at a pace that maximizes your performance at the marathon, you will be faster than ever. And by running at your marathon heart rate, you will find this sweet spot.

Training schedules explained

The 14-kilometer (8.69 miles) schedule consists of four workouts per week, with two "long" workouts, starting at 10 (6.21 miles) kilometers and increasing to a maximum of 14 kilometers (8.69 miles).

You do one interval training session. You will do one easy run a week. Just run quietly, and enjoy your surroundings a bit. And two training sessions, during which you run at marathon heart rate. The four workouts are fixed. The speed at which you run and your heart rate vary from person to person.

In the diagram on the following pages, you will see a resting pulse in the first column. There, you can keep track of your resting heart rate to help you determine whether you are recovered. More on that later. Take a look at the accumulation of the mileage over the past hundred days.

It's a 100-day marathon schedule, which is a little over fourteen weeks. The schedule starts on the fifth day of the week. Because if you start with a hundred days on Friday, then the hundredth day is a Sunday. And most marathons are on Sundays.

As you can see in the diagram, it is not a simple training plan. Runners who think they can easily "tick off" the marathon with the schedule will be disappointed. You train 497 kilometers (308.82 miles) in 100 days, and you train with attention and dedication focused on heart rate (or pace). More on that later.

Marathon pace and Heart rate

The most important part of the entire schedule is your marathon heart rate; you train the most at this intensity level.

You can follow the schedule in two ways:

- Marathon pace

- Marathon heart rate

My advice is to run at a marathon heart rate, which I will discuss in more detail later. However, it is also possible to follow the schedule at marathon pace.

How do you determine your marathon pace?

The marathon contains a comparison table of performances at different distances. The times are indicated in hours, minutes, and seconds.

If you have run 10 kilometers at full speed in the last six months, you can, approximately, predict your marathon time. If you have run different distances, you probably noticed that they are not all on the same line. For example, if you run 10 kilometers at 53:32 and run the marathon at 4:16:42, you will see that your marathon time is faster than you expect based on your 10 kilometers. After all, the table states that your expected marathon time is 4:31:27 based on a 10-kilometer time of 53:32.

That can mean two things. Or you simply have more talent for longer distances, or, and that is very likely, you can do better on the 10 kilometers. Because running a fast 10 kilometers is difficult and your muscles will ache.

Predict your marathon time
The table below shows a prediction of your marathon time based on 10 kilometers that you run as fast as possible.

10K time	Predicted Marathon time
1:04:34	5:39:51
1:02:45	5:28:14
1:01:01	5:17:20
59:23	5:07:04
57:49	4:57:25

56:19	4:48:16
54:53	4:39:38
53:32	4:31:27
52:13	4:23:42
50:58	4:16:20
49:46	4:09:19
48:36	4:02:39
47:31	3:56:17
46:27	3:50:13
45:25	3:44:25
44:26	3:38:53
43:30	3:33:35
42:35	3:28:30
41:42	3:23:38
40:51	3.18.58
40:02	3:14:29
39:15	3:10:10
38:29	3:06:01
37:44	3:02:02
37:02	2:58:12

For a 10-kilometer time over 65 minutes, the expected marathon time is 5:52:13 or longer. I recommend that people who take 10 kilometers for longer than 65 minutes improve their 10-kilometer time first. If that doesn't work, you can of course train for a marathon, but then I recommend a personal schedule and not the one in this book.

For a 10-kilometer time under 37 minutes, the expected marathon time is 2:54:30 or faster. People who want to run faster than 2:54:30 in the marathon are advised to follow a personal schedule, and not the one in this book.

Training on marathon heart rate

I already wrote that I favor training based on marathon heart rate instead of marathon pace. Training based on heart rate ensures that physical changes or other weather conditions do not negatively affect the training load. Because if, for example, you are under a lot of stress or there is a strong wind, your pace will drop, ensuring you apply the correct training load. However, if you train at a predetermined pace, your training load will be higher than it should be, because your body will need to work harder to sustain the predetermined pace.

Running at marathon speed is also not without risk on the day of the marathon itself. Again, we have the example of 6.04 minutes per kilometer (9.45 minutes per mile). You trained for 99 days to complete the event with a finish time of 4:16. On the day of the marathon, it rained very hard and there was a lot of wind. If you then start with 6.04 minutes per kilometer (9.45 minutes per mile), it will be a tough day. It might go well up to 30 kilometers (18.64 miles). But after that, you will likely hit a wall. Because you ran too fast and your body doesn't have enough energy to finish in 4:16 due to the strong wind and rain.

You can prevent that problem by training and running your race according to your heart rate. Because if you run on your marathon heart rate, then your pace will drop if you have a strong headwind. Of course, your finish time will be slower, but that is due to circumstances beyond your control. You will likely be faster than when you run at a predetermined pace because your body's energy supply is used optimally.

How do you determine your marathon heart rate? I will now explain that.

You already know how to determine your anaerobic threshold. Moreover, you discovered how long you could run in each specific heart rate zone. Your expected finish time and anaerobic threshold determine your marathon heart rate.

That sounds logical, but it often goes wrong.

An example. Peter and Richard both have an anaerobic threshold of 180. Still, Peter's marathon heart rate is 176, and Richard's marathon heart rate is 131.

How is that possible?

Peter runs 10 kilometers in 28 minutes and runs the marathon at 2:12. Because he is extremely good and he only has to run for 2 hours, he can run at a high heart rate.

Richard does not run 10 kilometers in 28 minutes but in 65 minutes. His marathon heart rate is 131, much lower than Peter's because Richard needs to keep running for almost 6 hours.

Because fast runners will take less time to finish a marathon, they can train with a higher heart rate. This also explains why fast runners can also run more mileage. If you run the marathon in 2:10, then training for 30 kilometers (18.64 miles) is still only 1:40.

Note: It is impossible to run exactly at that heart rate for the entire run, and you don't have to. The trick is to run as much of your workouts as possible at that heart rate. You will probably notice that you sometimes have to slow down at the end of the run to stay within your marathon heart rate.

You make progress if you run faster at the same heart rate. A bonus is that it becomes more difficult to reach your maximum heart rate; you have to work harder for it. But that's a good sign.

What are the disadvantages of the proposed schedule?
I have explained how the training schedule works and what the benefits are. Are there any drawbacks to the schedule?

Long runs
I often get the question of why runners are no longer allowed to do long runs. Long-distance runners don't want to miss out on their favorite runs and wonder why they can't do it anymore. I have to laugh about that, because of course, I am not saying that you can no longer do long runs, it is just not necessary.

It is noticeable that many runners get injured or fatigued from their regular schedules, but if you can enjoy long runs without injury, you can safely continue to do so. The regular schedules have long proven themselves; after all, hundreds of thousands of runners have run marathons with them, so if you like that schedule, you can keep doing it. The 14-kilometer training schedule is an alternative for people who are injured from the strenuous training weeks or for people who prefer not to do the long runs.

Psychologically tough
Many runners also have difficulty with uncertainty. With a maximum training distance of 14 kilometers (8.69 miles), the marathon distance seems too far. "Can I do it?" Runners wonder. The schedule has worked for many others, but you can still doubt whether it is right for you. And how do you deal with that mentally?

I fooled myself with a psychological trick that professionals use as well. At the start, I focused on the first 14 kilometers (8.69 miles), as I had done so many times before in training. After 14 kilometers (8.69 miles), I said to myself, "Now again, 14 kilometers (8.69 miles)." Then I was already at 28 kilometers (17.39 miles), and I said to myself, "Only 14 kilometers (8.69

miles) to the finish." And so I ran 14 kilometers (8.69 miles) to the finish three times.

It does not work that way for everyone. In the last week before the marathon, I often get people on the phone who are unsure, and that is not surprising. Runners who are members of an athletics association and who are the only ones who follow this schedule have a hard time. If you are still only running 14 kilometers (8.69 miles) three weeks before the marathon, while the entire club is already training for more than 30 kilometers (18.64 miles), you can become insecure. Especially if the other runners think you are crazy and don't believe in the schedule. Doubt always backfires, so it is important to remember that it is possible.

Trust is very powerful. In a science program, Diederik Jekel once performed a psychological test in the run-up to his marathon. One of the results was striking: by simply repeating "I can do it," "I can do it," he ran a lot better. Regardless of his real thoughts, just repeating these words was enough.

Physiologically, you can prepare for a marathon with the schedule; the tips are only meant to keep the courage psychological.

Injury sensitivity

I am also often asked whether the schedule is not prone to injury. Shouldn't you also train your ligaments and joints, and is 14 kilometers of training enough to do that?

Regular schedules are much more prone to injury due to the overload, as Maarten Fornerod's study showed. According to his study, injuries are mainly the result of running too far and not recovering enough.

After a run, your body recovers at least on three different levels: that of your breathing, the energy stores in your muscles, and the tendons, ligaments, and joints. Your breathing recovery is by far the fastest. Immediately after running, the breathing calms down again, which takes less than two minutes. The energy stores in your muscles need longer than two minutes. Your energy stores are replenished in 24 to 48 hours after normal training, depending on your fitness level. After a tough competition, for example, the recovery is 72 hours. If you look at tendons, ligaments, and joints, they sometimes take weeks or months to recover from a hard or long workout, as Fornerod shows.

That is why it is so frustrating for some runners to notice that the long runs become increasingly difficult with the regular schedules. The first training of 30 kilometers (18.64 miles)

is fine. After two weeks, the energy supplies in the muscles are back to normal, but the tendons, ligaments, and joints have not fully recovered. That is why the second practice of more than 30 kilometers (18.64 miles) is a lot harder, and after that many runners get injured.

Which training schedule should you follow?

You can probably figure out which training schedule is the right fit for you. If you've never run before, it is unwise to start directly with the marathon schedule. As you've discovered in Chapter 1, correct training load and adequate recovery are vital, and your progress will be far from optimal.

If you are unsure which schedule is the right fit for you, I advise you to follow the first week of a training schedule that fits your goal. If your resting heart rate doesn't recover before your next training, I advise you to start with an easier schedule. I, for instance, set a goal to run a marathon. After my first week of training, my resting heart rate didn't recover fast enough. On 3 of the 4 training days in the first week, my heartbeat was still up by 7 beats. So I stepped down to a less intense schedule and first started with the half marathon training schedule. I ran it at the tempo of "running with a smile." My goal is to enjoy each run.

Chapter 6: Marathon schedule

You will find your marathon heart rate at the end of this chapter. Each interval session is focused on making your body adjust to higher speeds. You will find your interval pace at the end of this chapter. Remember that the time in between the intervals is as long as the interval itself takes. So if you need to run a 400-meter interval in 1.38-1.32, you will also rest just as long. I advise you to run in zones 1 or 2 during the resting period instead of walking or standing still. This will help your body adjust to being able to recover during a run, which you might need if you started running too fast during a race.

I recommend keeping track of your average pace, average heart rate, and average cadence, to make it possible to track your progress. If your average pace is faster with the same average heart rate, you are making progress. For those of you who want to print this schedule, I've made a PDF available on my website https://runbyheartrate.wordpress.com/trainingschedules/

Week 1

Resting Heart rate	KM	Tempo	Average pace	Average heart rate	Average cadence
	10	Marathon Heart rate			
	6	Interval (15x 400m)			

Week 2

Resting Heart rate	KM	Tempo	Average pace	Average heart rate	Average cadence
	9	Marathon			

		Heart rate			
	5	Z1			
	6	Interval (6x 1000m)			
	10	Marathon Heart rate			

Week 3

Resting Heart rate	KM	Tempo	Average pace	Average heart rate	Average cadence
	10	Marathon Heart rate			
	5	Z1			
	6	Interval (3x 2000m)			
	10	Marathon Heart rate			

Week 4

Resting Heart rate	KM	Tempo	Average pace	Average heart rate	Average cadence
	11	Marathon Heart rate			
	5	Z1			
	6	Interval (15 x 400m)			
	10	AT			

Week 5

Resting Heart rate	KM	Tempo	Average pace	Average heart rate	Average cadence
	5	Z1			
	12	Marathon Heart rate			
	6	Interval (6x 1000m)			
	10	Marathon Heart rate			

Week 6

Resting Heart rate	KM	Tempo	Average pace	Average heart rate	Average cadence
	12	Marathon Heart rate			
	6	Z1			
	7	Interval (3x 2000m + 1000m)			
	10	Marathon Heart rate			

Week 7

Resting Heart rate	KM	Tempo	Average pace	Average heart rate	Average cadence
	12	Marathon Heart rate			
	6	Z1			

	6	Interval (15x 400m)			
	10	AT			

Week 8

Resting Heart rate	KM	Tempo	Average pace	Average heart rate	Average cadence
	6	Z1			
	12	Marathon Heart rate			
	7	Interval (7x 1000m)			
	12	Marathon Heart rate			

Week 9

Resting Heart rate	KM	Tempo	Average pace	Average heart rate	Average cadence
	6	Z1			
	12	Marathon Heart rate			
	6	Interval (3x 2000m)			
	12	Marathon Heart rate			

Week 10

Resting	KM	Tempo	Average	Average	Average

Heart rate			pace	heart rate	cadence
	13	Marathon Heart rate			
	7	Interval (7 x 1000m)			
	6	Z1			
	10	AT			

Week 11

Resting Heart rate	KM	Tempo	Average pace	Average heart rate	Average cadence
	7	Z1			
	14	Marathon Heart rate			
	9	Interval (3x 2000m +1000m)			
	12	Marathon Heart rate			

Week 12

Resting Heart rate	KM	Tempo	Average pace	Average heart rate	Average cadence
	7	Z1			
	14	Marathon Heart rate			
	8	Interval (8x 1000m)			
	12	Marathon Heart rate			

Week 13 (toughest week)

Resting Heart rate	KM	Tempo	Average pace	Average heart rate	Average cadence
	14	Marathon Heart rate			
	9	Interval (4x 2000m + 1000m)			
	7	Z1			
	14	AT			

Week 14

Resting Heart rate	KM	Tempo	Average pace	Average heart rate	Average cadence
	7	Z1			
	14	Marathon Heart rate			
	8	Interval (8 x1000m)			
	6	Marathon Heart rate			

Week 15 (Tapering of training load for best performance)

Resting Heart rate	KM	Tempo	Average pace	Average heart rate	Average cadence
	12	Marathon Heart rate			

	12 min	Marathon tempo			
	12 min	Marathon tempo			
	MARATHON				

Nutrition for the marathon

How much you need to drink and eat during the marathon to minimize dehydration depends on your body size and pace, the heat and humidity, and your sweat rate. The maximum amount you should drink while running is the amount your stomach can empty or the amount you've lost as sweat, whichever is less. You should drink enough during the marathon so you don't lose more than about 2 to 3 percent of your body weight during the race. Drinking more than you've lost increases the risk of hyponatremia.

Research has shown that most runners' stomachs can empty only about 180 to 210 ml (6 to 7 ounces) of fluid every 15 minutes during running, which represents about 720 to 840 ml (24 to 28 ounces) per hour. If you drink more than that, the extra fluid will slosh around in your stomach and not provide any additional benefit. You may need more or less than the average, so experiment with how much liquid and food your stomach can tolerate at a race pace. During running, it is very difficult to drink 200 ml of fluid at an aid station without stopping, and a 2007 study by Dr. Tim Noakes and colleagues found that most runners drink less than 480 ml (16 ounces) per hour when racing. But drinking and eating too little can certainly hamper your performance. It can easily cost you 30 minutes. So if you have trouble eating and drinking while running, I advise you to stop for a few seconds. This will take less time than the time you lose by not eating and drinking.

Moreover, I strongly advise you to practice drinking and eating during at least 2 training sessions. My stomach becomes upset after taking a gel, so instead, I take Gatorade as a drink and eat winegums. The advantage of Gatorade is that it also contains calories, so I still get enough calories, especially carbohydrates.

Time or distance	Nutrition
1 hour prior to the race	500 ml of liquid (17 ounces)
10K	Gel (100 calories)
15K	Water cup (250ml) (8 ounces)
20K	Gel (100 calories)
25K	Water cup (250ml) (17 ounces)
30K	Gel (100 calories)
35K	Water cup (250 ml) (8 ounces)
40K	Water cup (250ml) (8 ounces)

Interval Pace

10K time	Anaerobic threshold	2000m interval	1000m interval	400m interval	200m interval
30	3.09-3.04	7.00-6.30	3.23-3.08	1.15-1.09	34-31
31	3.15-3.10	7.12-6.42	3.29-3.14	1.17-1.11	35-32
32	3.21-3.16	7.24-6.54	3.35-3.20	1.19-1.13	36-33
33	3.27-3.22	7.36-7.06	3.41-3.26	1.22-1.16	37-33
34	3.33-3.28	7.48-7.18	3.47-3.32	1.24-1.18	38-33
35	3.39-3.34	8.00-7.30	3.53-3.38	1.26-1.20	38-34
36	3.45-3.40	8.12-7.42	3.59-3.44	1.29-1.23	39-35
37	3.51-3.46	8.24-7.54	4.05-3.50	1.31-1.25	40-36
38	3.57-3.52	8.36-8.06	4.11-3.56	1.33-1.27	41-36
39	4.03-3.58	8.48-8.18	4.17-4.02	1.36-1.30	42-37
40	4.09-4.04	9.00-8.30	4.23-4.08	1.38-1.32	43-38
41	4.15-4.10	9.12-8.42	4.29-4.14	1.40-1.34	44-48
42	4.21-.4.16	9.24-8.54	4.35-4.20	1.43-1.37	44-39
43	4.27-4.22	9.36-9.06	4.41-4.26	1.45-1.39	45-40
44	4.33-4.28	9.48-9.18	4.47-4.32	1.47-1.41	46-41
45	4.39-4.34	10.00-9.30	4.53-4.38	1.50-1.43	47-42

46	4.45-4.40	10.12-9.42	4.59-4.44	1.52-1.45	48-43
47	4.51-4.46	10.24-9.54	5.05-4.50	1.53-1.47	48-44
48	4.57-4.52	10.36-10.06	5.11-4.56	1.56-1.50	49-45
49	5.03-4.58	10.48-10.18	5.17-5.02	1.58-1.52	50-46
50	5.09-5.04	11.00-10.30	5.23-5.08	2.00-1.54	52-48
51	5.15-5.10	11.12-10.42	5.29-5.14	2.03-1.57	53-49
52	5.21-5.16	11.24-10.54	5.35-5.20	2.05-1.59	54-50
53	5.25 5.20	11.36-11.06	5.41-5.26	2.07-2.01	55-51
54	5.29-5.24	11.48-11.18	5.47-5.32	2.10-2.04	56-52
55	5.30	12.00-11.30	5.53-5.38	2.12-2.06	57-53
56	5.36	12.12-11.42	5.59-5.44	2.14-2.08	58-54
57	5.42	11.24 11.54	6.05-5.50	2.17-2.11	59-55
58	5.48	11.36-12.06	6.11-5.56	2.19-2.13	60-56
59	5.54	12.48-12.18	6.17-6.02	2.21-2.15	61-57
60	6.00	13.00-12.30	6.23-6.08	2.24-2.18	62-58
61	6.06	13.12-12.42	6.29-6.14	2.27-2.21	63-59
62	6.12	13.24-12.54	6.35-6.20	2.30-2.24	64-60
63	6.18	13.36-13.06	6.41-6.26	2.33-2.27	65-61

| 64 | 6.24 | 13.48-13.18 | 6.47-6.32 | 2.37-2.30 | 66-62 |
| 65 | 6.30 | 14.00-13.30 | 6.54-6.38 | 2.40-2.33 | 67-63 |

Marathon Heart rate

Anaerobic threshold	10K time	Marathon Heart rate
139	30	131
	31	130
	32	129
	33	128
	34	127
	35	126
	36	125
	37	124
	38	123
	39	122
	40	121
	41	120
	42	119
	43	118
	44	117
	45	116
	46	115
	47	114
	48	113
	49	112
	50	111
	51	110
	52	109
	53	108

	54	107
	55	106
	56	105
	57	104
	58	103
	59	102
	60	101
	61	100
	62	99
	63	98
	64	97
	65	96

Anaerobic threshold	10K time	Marathon Heart rate
140	30	132
	31	131
	32	130
	33	129
	34	128
	35	127
	36	126
	37	125
	38	124
	39	123
	40	122
	41	121
	42	120
	43	119
	44	118
	45	117
	46	116
	47	115

		48	114
		49	113
		50	112
		51	111
		52	110
		53	109
		54	108
		55	107
		56	106
		57	105
		58	104
		59	103
		60	102
		61	101
		62	100
		63	99
		64	98
		65	97

Anaerobic threshold	10K time	Marathon Heart rate
141	30	133
	31	132
	32	131
	33	130
	34	129
	35	128
	36	127
	37	126
	38	125
	39	124
	40	123
	41	122

		42	121
		43	120
		44	119
		45	118
		46	117
		47	116
		48	115
		49	114
		50	113
		51	112
		52	111
		53	110
		54	109
		55	108
		56	107
		57	106
		58	105
		59	104
		60	103
		61	102
		62	101
		63	100
		64	99
		65	98

Anaerobic threshold	10K time	Marathon Heart rate
142	30	134
	31	133
	32	132
	33	131
	34	130
	35	129
	36	128
	37	127
	38	126
	39	125
	40	124
	41	123
	42	122
	43	121
	44	120
	45	119
	46	118
	47	117
	48	116
	49	115
	50	114
	51	113
	52	112
	53	111
	54	110
	55	109
	56	108
	57	107
	58	106
	59	105
	60	104
	61	103

		62	102
		63	101
		64	100
		65	99

Anaerobic threshold	10K time	Marathon Heart rate
143	30	135
	31	134
	32	133
	33	132
	34	131
	35	130
	36	129
	37	128
	38	127
	39	126
	40	125
	41	124
	42	123
	43	122
	44	121
	45	120
	46	119
	47	118
	48	117
	49	116
	50	115
	51	114
	52	113
	53	112
	54	111
	55	110

	56	109
	57	108
	58	107
	59	106
	60	105
	61	104
	62	103
	63	102
	64	101
	65	100

Anaerobic threshold	10K time	Marathon Heart rate
144	30	136
	31	135
	32	134
	33	133
	34	132
	35	131
	36	130
	37	129
	38	128
	39	127
	40	126
	41	125
	42	124
	43	123
	44	122
	45	121
	46	120
	47	119
	48	118
	49	117

		50	116
		51	115
		52	114
		53	113
		54	112
		55	111
		56	110
		57	109
		58	108
		59	107
		60	106
		61	105
		62	104
		63	103
		64	102
		65	101

Anaerobic threshold	10K time	Marathon Heart rate
145	30	137
	31	136
	32	135
	33	134
	34	133
	35	132
	36	131
	37	130
	38	129
	39	128
	40	127
	41	126
	42	125
	43	124

	44	123
	45	122
	46	121
	47	120
	48	119
	49	118
	50	117
	51	116
	52	115
	53	114
	54	113
	55	112
	56	111
	57	110
	58	109
	59	108
	60	107
	61	106
	62	105
	63	104
	64	103
	65	102

Anaerobic threshold	10K time	Marathon Heart rate
146	30	138
	31	137
	32	136
	33	135
	34	134
	35	133
	36	132
	37	131

		38	130
		39	129
		40	128
		41	127
		42	126
		43	125
		44	124
		45	123
		46	122
		47	121
		48	120
		49	119
		50	118
		51	117
		52	116
		53	115
		54	114
		55	113
		56	112
		57	111
		58	110
		59	109
		60	108
		61	107
		62	106
		63	105
		64	104
		65	103

Anaerobic threshold	10K time	Marathon Heart rate
147	30	139
	31	138

	32	137
	33	136
	34	135
	35	134
	36	133
	37	132
	38	131
	39	130
	40	129
	41	128
	42	127
	43	126
	44	125
	45	124
	46	123
	47	122
	48	121
	49	120
	50	119
	51	118
	52	117
	53	116
	54	115
	55	114
	56	113
	57	112
	58	111
	59	110
	60	109
	61	108
	62	107
	63	106
	64	105

	65	104

Anaerobic threshold	10K time	Marathon Heart rate
148	30	140
	31	139
	32	138
	33	137
	34	136
	35	135
	36	134
	37	133
	38	132
	39	131
	40	130
	41	129
	42	128
	43	127
	44	126
	45	125
	46	124
	47	123
	48	122
	49	121
	50	120
	51	119
	52	118
	53	117
	54	116
	55	115
	56	114
	57	113
	58	112

		59	111
		60	110
		61	109
		62	108
		63	107
		64	106
		65	105

Anaerobic threshold	10K time		Marathon Heart rate
149	30		141
	31		140
	32		139
	33		138
	34		137
	35		136
	36		135
	37		134
	38		133
	39		132
	40		131
	41		130
	42		129
	43		128
	44		127
	45		126
	46		125
	47		124
	48		123
	49		122
	50		121
	51		120
	52		119

	53	118
	54	117
	55	116
	56	115
	57	114
	58	113
	59	112
	60	111
	61	110
	62	109
	63	108
	64	107
	65	106

Anaerobic threshold	10K time	Marathon Heart rate
150	30	142
	31	141
	32	140
	33	139
	34	138
	35	137
	36	136
	37	135
	38	134
	39	133
	40	132
	41	131
	42	130
	43	129
	44	128
	45	127
	46	126

		47	125
		48	124
		49	123
		50	122
		51	121
		52	120
		53	119
		54	118
		55	117
		56	116
		57	115
		58	114
		59	113
		60	112
		61	111
		62	110
		63	109
		64	108
		65	107

Anaerobic threshold	10K time	Marathon Heart rate
151	30	143
	31	142
	32	141
	33	140
	34	139
	35	138
	36	137
	37	136
	38	135
	39	134
	40	133

	41	132
	42	131
	43	130
	44	129
	45	128
	46	127
	47	126
	48	125
	49	124
	50	123
	51	122
	52	121
	53	120
	54	119
	55	118
	56	117
	57	116
	58	115
	59	114
	60	113
	61	112
	62	111
	63	110
	64	109
	65	108

Anaerobic threshold	10K time	Marathon Heart rate
152	30	144
	31	143
	32	142
	33	141
	34	140

	35	139
	36	138
	37	137
	38	136
	39	135
	40	134
	41	133
	42	132
	43	131
	44	130
	45	129
	46	128
	47	127
	48	126
	49	125
	50	124
	51	123
	52	122
	53	121
	54	120
	55	119
	56	118
	57	117
	58	116
	59	115
	60	114
	61	113
	62	112
	63	111
	64	110
	65	109

Anaerobic	10K time	Marathon Heart

threshold		rate	
153	30		145
	31		144
	32		143
	33		142
	34		141
	35		140
	36		139
	37		138
	38		137
	39		136
	40		135
	41		134
	42		133
	43		132
	44		131
	45		130
	46		129
	47		128
	48		127
	49		126
	50		125
	51		124
	52		123
	53		122
	54		121
	55		120
	56		119
	57		118
	58		117
	59		116
	60		115
	61		114
	62		113

		63	112
		64	111
		65	110

Anaerobic threshold	10K time	Marathon Heart rate
154	30	146
	31	145
	32	144
	33	143
	34	142
	35	141
	36	140
	37	139
	38	138
	39	137
	40	136
	41	135
	42	134
	43	133
	44	132
	45	131
	46	130
	47	129
	48	128
	49	127
	50	126
	51	125
	52	124
	53	123
	54	122
	55	121
	56	120

		57	119
		58	118
		59	117
		60	116
		61	115
		62	114
		63	113
		64	112
		65	111

Anaerobic threshold	10K time	Marathon Heart rate
155	30	147
	31	146
	32	145
	33	144
	34	143
	35	142
	36	141
	37	140
	38	139
	39	138
	40	137
	41	136
	42	135
	43	134
	44	133
	45	132
	46	131
	47	130
	48	129
	49	128
	50	127

		51	126
		52	125
		53	124
		54	123
		55	122
		56	121
		57	120
		58	119
		59	118
		60	117
		61	116
		62	115
		63	114
		64	113
		65	112

Anaerobic threshold	10K time	Marathon Heart rate
156	30	148
	31	147
	32	146
	33	145
	34	144
	35	143
	36	142
	37	141
	38	140
	39	139
	40	138
	41	137
	42	136
	43	135
	44	134

	45	133
	46	132
	47	131
	48	130
	49	129
	50	128
	51	127
	52	126
	53	125
	54	124
	55	123
	56	122
	57	121
	58	120
	59	119
	60	118
	61	117
	62	116
	63	115
	64	114
	65	113

Anaerobic threshold	10K time	Marathon Heart rate
157	30	149
	31	148
	32	147
	33	146
	34	145
	35	144
	36	143
	37	142
	38	141

	39	140
	40	139
	41	138
	42	137
	43	136
	44	135
	45	134
	46	133
	47	132
	48	131
	49	130
	50	129
	51	128
	52	127
	53	126
	54	125
	55	124
	56	123
	57	122
	58	121
	59	120
	60	119
	61	118
	62	117
	63	116
	64	115
	65	114

Anaerobic threshold	10K time	Marathon Heart rate
158	30	150
	31	149
	32	148

	33	147
	34	146
	35	145
	36	144
	37	143
	38	142
	39	141
	40	140
	41	139
	42	138
	43	137
	44	136
	45	135
	46	134
	47	133
	48	132
	49	131
	50	130
	51	129
	52	128
	53	127
	54	126
	55	125
	56	124
	57	123
	58	122
	59	121
	60	120
	61	119
	62	118
	63	117
	64	116
	65	115

Anaerobic threshold	10K time	Marathon Heart rate
159	30	151
	31	150
	32	149
	33	148
	34	147
	35	146
	36	145
	37	144
	38	143
	39	142
	40	141
	41	140
	42	139
	43	138
	44	137
	45	136
	46	135
	47	134
	48	133
	49	132
	50	131
	51	130
	52	129
	53	128
	54	127
	55	126
	56	125
	57	124
	58	123
	59	122
	60	121
	61	120

	62	119
	63	118
	64	117
	65	116

Anaerobic threshold	10K time	Marathon Heart rate
160	30	152
	31	151
	32	150
	33	149
	34	148
	35	147
	36	146
	37	145
	38	144
	39	143
	40	142
	41	141
	42	140
	43	139
	44	138
	45	137
	46	136
	47	135
	48	134
	49	133
	50	132
	51	131
	52	130
	53	129
	54	128
	55	127

		56	126
		57	125
		58	124
		59	123
		60	122
		61	121
		62	120
		63	119
		64	118
		65	117

Anaerobic threshold	10K time	Marathon Heart rate
161	30	153
	31	152
	32	151
	33	150
	34	149
	35	148
	36	147
	37	146
	38	145
	39	144
	40	143
	41	142
	42	141
	43	140
	44	139
	45	138
	46	137
	47	136
	48	135
	49	134

	50	133
	51	132
	52	131
	53	130
	54	129
	55	128
	56	127
	57	126
	58	125
	59	124
	60	123
	61	122
	62	121
	63	120
	64	119
	65	118

Anaerobic threshold	10K time	Marathon Heart rate
162	30	154
	31	153
	32	152
	33	151
	34	150
	35	149
	36	148
	37	147
	38	146
	39	145
	40	144
	41	143
	42	142
	43	141

		44	140
		45	139
		46	138
		47	137
		48	136
		49	135
		50	134
		51	133
		52	132
		53	131
		54	130
		55	129
		56	128
		57	127
		58	126
		59	125
		60	124
		61	123
		62	122
		63	121
		64	120
		65	119

Anaerobic threshold	10K time	Marathon Heart rate
163	30	155
	31	154
	32	153
	33	152
	34	151
	35	150
	36	149
	37	148

	38	147
	39	146
	40	145
	41	144
	42	143
	43	142
	44	141
	45	140
	46	139
	47	138
	48	137
	49	136
	50	135
	51	134
	52	133
	53	132
	54	131
	55	130
	56	129
	57	128
	58	127
	59	126
	60	125
	61	124
	62	123
	63	122
	64	121
	65	120

Anaerobic threshold	10K time	Marathon Heart rate
164	30	156
	31	155

	32	154
	33	153
	34	152
	35	151
	36	150
	37	149
	38	148
	39	147
	40	146
	41	145
	42	144
	43	143
	44	142
	45	141
	46	140
	47	139
	48	138
	49	137
	50	136
	51	135
	52	134
	53	133
	54	132
	55	131
	56	130
	57	129
	58	128
	59	127
	60	126
	61	125
	62	124
	63	123
	64	122

		65	121

Anaerobic threshold	10K time	Marathon Heart rate
165	30	157
	31	156
	32	155
	33	154
	34	153
	35	152
	36	151
	37	150
	38	149
	39	148
	40	147
	41	146
	42	145
	43	144
	44	143
	45	142
	46	141
	47	140
	48	139
	49	138
	50	137
	51	136
	52	135
	53	134
	54	133
	55	132
	56	131
	57	130
	58	129

		59	128
		60	127
		61	126
		62	125
		63	124
		64	123
		65	122

Anaerobic threshold	10K time	Marathon Heart rate
166	30	158
	31	157
	32	156
	33	155
	34	154
	35	153
	36	152
	37	151
	38	150
	39	149
	40	148
	41	147
	42	146
	43	145
	44	144
	45	143
	46	142
	47	141
	48	140
	49	139
	50	138
	51	137
	52	136

		53	135
		54	134
		55	133
		56	132
		57	131
		58	130
		59	129
		60	128
		61	127
		62	126
		63	125
		64	124
		65	123

Anaerobic threshold	10K time	Marathon Heart rate
167	30	159
	31	158
	32	157
	33	156
	34	155
	35	154
	36	153
	37	152
	38	151
	39	150
	40	149
	41	148
	42	147
	43	146
	44	145
	45	144
	46	143

		47	142
		48	141
		49	140
		50	139
		51	138
		52	137
		53	136
		54	135
		55	134
		56	133
		57	132
		58	131
		59	130
		60	129
		61	128
		62	127
		63	126
		64	125
		65	124

Anaerobic threshold	10K time	Marathon Heart rate
168	30	160
	31	159
	32	158
	33	157
	34	156
	35	155
	36	154
	37	153
	38	152
	39	151
	40	150

		41	149
		42	148
		43	147
		44	146
		45	145
		46	144
		47	143
		48	142
		49	141
		50	140
		51	139
		52	138
		53	137
		54	136
		55	135
		56	134
		57	133
		58	132
		59	131
		60	130
		61	129
		62	128
		63	127
		64	126
		65	125

Anaerobic threshold	10K time	Marathon Heart rate
169	30	161
	31	160
	32	159
	33	158
	34	157

		35	156
		36	155
		37	154
		38	153
		39	152
		40	151
		41	150
		42	149
		43	148
		44	147
		45	146
		46	145
		47	144
		48	143
		49	142
		50	141
		51	140
		52	139
		53	138
		54	137
		55	136
		56	135
		57	134
		58	133
		59	132
		60	131
		61	130
		62	129
		63	128
		64	127
		65	126

Anaerobic	10K time	Marathon Heart

threshold		rate	
170	30		162
	31		161
	32		160
	33		159
	34		158
	35		157
	36		156
	37		155
	38		154
	39		153
	40		152
	41		151
	42		150
	43		149
	44		148
	45		147
	46		146
	47		145
	48		144
	49		143
	50		142
	51		141
	52		140
	53		139
	54		138
	55		137
	56		136
	57		135
	58		134
	59		133
	60		132
	61		131
	62		130

		63	129
		64	128
		65	127

Anaerobic threshold	10K time	Marathon Heart rate
171	30	163
	31	162
	32	161
	33	160
	34	159
	35	158
	36	157
	37	156
	38	155
	39	154
	40	153
	41	152
	42	151
	43	150
	44	149
	45	148
	46	147
	47	146
	48	145
	49	144
	50	143
	51	142
	52	141
	53	140
	54	139
	55	138
	56	137

	57	136
	58	135
	59	134
	60	133
	61	132
	62	131
	63	130
	64	129
	65	128

Anaerobic threshold	10K time	Marathon Heart rate
172	30	164
	31	163
	32	162
	33	161
	34	160
	35	159
	36	158
	37	157
	38	156
	39	155
	40	154
	41	153
	42	152
	43	151
	44	150
	45	149
	46	148
	47	147
	48	146
	49	145
	50	144

		51	143
		52	142
		53	141
		54	140
		55	139
		56	138
		57	137
		58	136
		59	135
		60	134
		61	133
		62	132
		63	131
		64	130
		65	129

Anaerobic threshold	10K time	Marathon Heart rate
173	30	165
	31	164
	32	163
	33	162
	34	161
	35	160
	36	159
	37	158
	38	157
	39	156
	40	155
	41	154
	42	153
	43	152
	44	151

	45	150
	46	149
	47	148
	48	147
	49	146
	50	145
	51	144
	52	143
	53	142
	54	141
	55	140
	56	139
	57	138
	58	137
	59	136
	60	135
	61	134
	62	133
	63	132
	64	131
	65	130

Anaerobic threshold	10K time	Marathon Heart rate
174	30	166
	31	165
	32	164
	33	163
	34	162
	35	161
	36	160
	37	159
	38	158

	39	157
	40	156
	41	155
	42	154
	43	153
	44	152
	45	151
	46	150
	47	149
	48	148
	49	147
	50	146
	51	145
	52	144
	53	143
	54	142
	55	141
	56	140
	57	139
	58	138
	59	137
	60	136
	61	135
	62	134
	63	133
	64	132
	65	131

Anaerobic threshold	10K time	Marathon Heart rate
175	30	167
	31	166
	32	165

		33	164
		34	163
		35	162
		36	161
		37	160
		38	159
		39	158
		40	157
		41	156
		42	155
		43	154
		44	153
		45	152
		46	151
		47	150
		48	149
		49	148
		50	147
		51	146
		52	145
		53	144
		54	143
		55	142
		56	141
		57	140
		58	139
		59	138
		60	137
		61	136
		62	135
		63	134
		64	133
		65	132

Anaerobic threshold	10K time	Marathon Heart rate
176	30	168
	31	167
	32	166
	33	165
	34	164
	35	163
	36	162
	37	161
	38	160
	39	159
	40	158
	41	157
	42	156
	43	155
	44	154
	45	153
	46	152
	47	151
	48	150
	49	149
	50	148
	51	147
	52	146
	53	145
	54	144
	55	143
	56	142
	57	141
	58	140
	59	139
	60	138
	61	137

	62	136
	63	135
	64	134
	65	133

Anaerobic threshold	10K time	Marathon Heart rate
177	30	169
	31	168
	32	167
	33	166
	34	165
	35	164
	36	163
	37	162
	38	161
	39	160
	40	159
	41	158
	42	157
	43	156
	44	155
	45	154
	46	153
	47	152
	48	151
	49	150
	50	149
	51	148
	52	147
	53	146
	54	145
	55	144

		56	143
		57	142
		58	141
		59	140
		60	139
		61	138
		62	137
		63	136
		64	135
		65	134

Anaerobic threshold	10K time	Marathon Heart rate
178	30	170
	31	169
	32	168
	33	167
	34	166
	35	165
	36	164
	37	163
	38	162
	39	161
	40	160
	41	159
	42	158
	43	157
	44	156
	45	155
	46	154
	47	153
	48	152
	49	151

	50	150
	51	149
	52	148
	53	147
	54	146
	55	145
	56	144
	57	143
	58	142
	59	141
	60	140
	61	139
	62	138
	63	137
	64	136
	65	135

Anaerobic threshold	10K time	Marathon Heart rate
179	30	171
	31	170
	32	169
	33	168
	34	167
	35	166
	36	165
	37	164
	38	163
	39	162
	40	161
	41	160
	42	159
	43	158

	44	157
	45	156
	46	155
	47	154
	48	153
	49	152
	50	151
	51	150
	52	149
	53	148
	54	147
	55	146
	56	145
	57	144
	58	143
	59	142
	60	141
	61	140
	62	139
	63	138
	64	137
	65	136

Anaerobic threshold	10K time	Marathon Heart rate
180	30	172
	31	171
	32	170
	33	169
	34	168
	35	167
	36	166
	37	165

		38	164
		39	163
		40	162
		41	161
		42	160
		43	159
		44	158
		45	157
		46	156
		47	155
		48	154
		49	153
		50	152
		51	151
		52	150
		53	149
		54	148
		55	147
		56	146
		57	145
		58	144
		59	143
		60	142
		61	141
		62	140
		63	139
		64	138
		65	137

Anaerobic threshold	10K time	Marathon Heart rate
181	30	173
	31	172

	32	171
	33	170
	34	169
	35	168
	36	167
	37	166
	38	165
	39	164
	40	163
	41	162
	42	161
	43	160
	44	159
	45	158
	46	157
	47	156
	48	155
	49	154
	50	153
	51	152
	52	151
	53	150
	54	149
	55	148
	56	147
	57	146
	58	145
	59	144
	60	143
	61	142
	62	141
	63	140
	64	139

	65	138

Anaerobic threshold	10K time	Marathon Heart rate
182	30	174
	31	173
	32	172
	33	171
	34	170
	35	169
	36	168
	37	167
	38	166
	39	165
	40	164
	41	163
	42	162
	43	161
	44	160
	45	159
	46	158
	47	157
	48	156
	49	155
	50	154
	51	153
	52	152
	53	151
	54	150
	55	149
	56	148
	57	147
	58	146

		59	145
		60	144
		61	143
		62	142
		63	141
		64	140
		65	139

Anaerobic threshold	10K time	Marathon Heart rate
183	30	175
	31	174
	32	173
	33	172
	34	171
	35	170
	36	169
	37	168
	38	167
	39	166
	40	165
	41	164
	42	163
	43	162
	44	161
	45	160
	46	159
	47	158
	48	157
	49	156
	50	155
	51	154
	52	153

	53	152
	54	151
	55	150
	56	149
	57	148
	58	147
	59	146
	60	145
	61	144
	62	143
	63	142
	64	141
	65	140

Anaerobic threshold	10K time	Marathon Heart rate
184	30	176
	31	175
	32	174
	33	173
	34	172
	35	171
	36	170
	37	169
	38	168
	39	167
	40	166
	41	165
	42	164
	43	163
	44	162
	45	161
	46	160

	47	159
	48	158
	49	157
	50	156
	51	155
	52	154
	53	153
	54	152
	55	151
	56	150
	57	149
	58	148
	59	147
	60	146
	61	145
	62	144
	63	143
	64	142
	65	141

Anaerobic threshold	10K time	Marathon Heart rate
185	30	177
	31	176
	32	175
	33	174
	34	173
	35	172
	36	171
	37	170
	38	169
	39	168
	40	167

		41	166
		42	165
		43	164
		44	163
		45	162
		46	161
		47	160
		48	159
		49	158
		50	157
		51	156
		52	155
		53	154
		54	153
		55	152
		56	151
		57	150
		58	149
		59	148
		60	147
		61	146
		62	145
		63	144
		64	143
		65	142

Anaerobic threshold	10K time	Marathon Heart rate
186	30	178
	31	177
	32	176
	33	175
	34	174

		35	173
		36	172
		37	171
		38	170
		39	169
		40	168
		41	167
		42	166
		43	165
		44	164
		45	163
		46	162
		47	161
		48	160
		49	159
		50	158
		51	157
		52	156
		53	155
		54	154
		55	153
		56	152
		57	151
		58	150
		59	149
		60	148
		61	147
		62	146
		63	145
		64	144
		65	143

Anaerobic	10K time	Marathon Heart

threshold		rate	
187	30		179
	31		178
	32		177
	33		176
	34		175
	35		174
	36		173
	37		172
	38		171
	39		170
	40		169
	41		168
	42		167
	43		166
	44		165
	45		164
	46		163
	47		162
	48		161
	49		160
	50		159
	51		158
	52		157
	53		156
	54		155
	55		154
	56		153
	57		152
	58		151
	59		150
	60		149
	61		148
	62		147

		63	146
		64	145
		65	144

Anaerobic threshold	10K time	Marathon Heart rate
188	30	180
	31	179
	32	178
	33	177
	34	176
	35	175
	36	174
	37	173
	38	172
	39	171
	40	170
	41	169
	42	168
	43	167
	44	166
	45	165
	46	164
	47	163
	48	162
	49	161
	50	160
	51	159
	52	158
	53	157
	54	156
	55	155
	56	154

	10K time	Marathon Heart rate
	57	153
	58	152
	59	151
	60	150
	61	149
	62	148
	63	147
	64	146
	65	145

Anaerobic threshold	10K time	Marathon Heart rate
189	30	181
	31	180
	32	179
	33	178
	34	177
	35	176
	36	175
	37	174
	38	173
	39	172
	40	171
	41	170
	42	169
	43	168
	44	167
	45	166
	46	165
	47	164
	48	163
	49	162
	50	161

		51	160
		52	159
		53	158
		54	157
		55	156
		56	155
		57	154
		58	153
		59	152
		60	151
		61	150
		62	149
		63	148
		64	147
		65	146

Anaerobic threshold	10K time	Marathon Heart rate
190	30	182
	31	181
	32	180
	33	179
	34	178
	35	177
	36	176
	37	175
	38	174
	39	173
	40	172
	41	171
	42	170
	43	169
	44	168

	45	167
	46	166
	47	165
	48	164
	49	163
	50	162
	51	161
	52	160
	53	159
	54	158
	55	157
	56	156
	57	155
	58	154
	59	153
	60	152
	61	151
	62	150
	63	149
	64	148
	65	147

Anaerobic threshold	10K time	Marathon Heart rate
191	30	183
	31	182
	32	181
	33	180
	34	179
	35	178
	36	177
	37	176
	38	175

		39	174
		40	173
		41	172
		42	171
		43	170
		44	169
		45	168
		46	167
		47	166
		48	165
		49	164
		50	163
		51	162
		52	161
		53	160
		54	159
		55	158
		56	157
		57	156
		58	155
		59	154
		60	153
		61	152
		62	151
		63	150
		64	149
		65	148

Anaerobic threshold	10K time	Marathon Heart rate
192	30	184
	31	183
	32	182

	33		181
	34		180
	35		179
	36		178
	37		177
	38		176
	39		175
	40		174
	41		173
	42		172
	43		171
	44		170
	45		169
	46		168
	47		167
	48		166
	49		165
	50		164
	51		163
	52		162
	53		161
	54		160
	55		159
	56		158
	57		157
	58		156
	59		155
	60		154
	61		153
	62		152
	63		151
	64		150
	65		149

Anaerobic threshold	10K time	Marathon Heart rate
193	30	185
	31	184
	32	183
	33	182
	34	181
	35	180
	36	179
	37	178
	38	177
	39	176
	40	175
	41	174
	42	173
	43	172
	44	171
	45	170
	46	169
	47	168
	48	167
	49	166
	50	165
	51	164
	52	163
	53	162
	54	161
	55	160
	56	159
	57	158
	58	157
	59	156
	60	155
	61	154

	62	153
	63	152
	64	151
	65	150

Anaerobic threshold	10K time	Marathon Heart rate
194	30	186
	31	185
	32	184
	33	183
	34	182
	35	181
	36	180
	37	179
	38	178
	39	177
	40	176
	41	175
	42	174
	43	173
	44	172
	45	171
	46	170
	47	169
	48	168
	49	167
	50	166
	51	165
	52	164
	53	163
	54	162
	55	161

	56	160
	57	159
	58	158
	59	157
	60	156
	61	155
	62	154
	63	153
	64	152
	65	151

Anaerobic threshold	10K time	Marathon Heart rate
195	30	187
	31	186
	32	185
	33	184
	34	183
	35	182
	36	181
	37	180
	38	179
	39	178
	40	177
	41	176
	42	175
	43	174
	44	173
	45	172
	46	171
	47	170
	48	169
	49	168

	50	167
	51	166
	52	165
	53	164
	54	163
	55	162
	56	161
	57	160
	58	159
	59	158
	60	157
	61	156
	62	155
	63	154
	64	153
	65	152

Anaerobic threshold	10K time	Marathon Heart rate
196	30	188
	31	187
	32	186
	33	185
	34	184
	35	183
	36	182
	37	181
	38	180
	39	179
	40	178
	41	177
	42	176
	43	175

	44	174
	45	173
	46	172
	47	171
	48	170
	49	169
	50	168
	51	167
	52	166
	53	165
	54	164
	55	163
	56	162
	57	161
	58	160
	59	159
	60	158
	61	157
	62	156
	63	155
	64	154
	65	153

Anaerobic threshold	10K time	Marathon Heart rate
197	30	189
	31	188
	32	187
	33	186
	34	185
	35	184
	36	183
	37	182

		38	181
		39	180
		40	179
		41	178
		42	177
		43	176
		44	175
		45	174
		46	173
		47	172
		48	171
		49	170
		50	169
		51	168
		52	167
		53	166
		54	165
		55	164
		56	163
		57	162
		58	161
		59	160
		60	159
		61	158
		62	157
		63	156
		64	155
		65	154

Anaerobic threshold	10K time	Marathon Heart rate	
198		30	190
		31	189

	32	188
	33	187
	34	186
	35	185
	36	184
	37	183
	38	182
	39	181
	40	180
	41	179
	42	178
	43	177
	44	176
	45	175
	46	174
	47	173
	48	172
	49	171
	50	170
	51	169
	52	168
	53	167
	54	166
	55	165
	56	164
	57	163
	58	162
	59	161
	60	160
	61	159
	62	158
	63	157
	64	156

		65	155

Anaerobic threshold	10K time	Marathon Heart rate
199	30	191
	31	190
	32	189
	33	188
	34	187
	35	186
	36	185
	37	184
	38	183
	39	182
	40	181
	41	180
	42	179
	43	178
	44	177
	45	176
	46	175
	47	174
	48	173
	49	172
	50	171
	51	170
	52	169
	53	168
	54	167
	55	166
	56	165
	57	164
	58	163

	59	162
	60	161
	61	160
	62	159
	63	158
	64	157
	65	156

Anaerobic threshold	10K time	Marathon Heart rate
200	30	192
	31	191
	32	190
	33	189
	34	188
	35	187
	36	186
	37	185
	38	184
	39	183
	40	182
	41	181
	42	180
	43	179
	44	178
	45	177
	46	176
	47	175
	48	174
	49	173
	50	172
	51	171
	52	170

	53	169
	54	168
	55	167
	56	166
	57	165
	58	164
	59	163
	60	162
	61	161
	62	160
	63	159
	64	158
	65	157

Anaerobic threshold	10K time	Marathon Heart rate
201	30	193
	31	192
	32	191
	33	190
	34	189
	35	188
	36	187
	37	186
	38	185
	39	184
	40	183
	41	182
	42	181
	43	180
	44	179
	45	178
	46	177

	47	176
	48	175
	49	174
	50	173
	51	172
	52	171
	53	170
	54	169
	55	168
	56	167
	57	166
	58	165
	59	164
	60	163
	61	162
	62	161
	63	160
	64	159
	65	158

Anaerobic threshold	10K time	Marathon Heart rate
202	30	194
	31	193
	32	192
	33	191
	34	190
	35	189
	36	188
	37	187
	38	186
	39	185
	40	184

	41	183
	42	182
	43	181
	44	180
	45	179
	46	178
	47	177
	48	176
	49	175
	50	174
	51	173
	52	172
	53	171
	54	170
	55	169
	56	168
	57	167
	58	166
	59	165
	60	164
	61	163
	62	162
	63	161
	64	160
	65	159

Anaerobic threshold	10K time	Marathon Heart rate
203	30	195
	31	194
	32	193
	33	192
	34	191

		35	190
		36	189
		37	188
		38	187
		39	186
		40	185
		41	184
		42	183
		43	182
		44	181
		45	180
		46	179
		47	178
		48	177
		49	176
		50	175
		51	174
		52	173
		53	172
		54	171
		55	170
		56	169
		57	168
		58	167
		59	166
		60	165
		61	164
		62	163
		63	162
		64	161
		65	160

Anaerobic	10K time	Marathon Heart

threshold		rate	
204	30	196	
	31	195	
	32	194	
	33	193	
	34	192	
	35	191	
	36	190	
	37	189	
	38	188	
	39	187	
	40	186	
	41	185	
	42	184	
	43	183	
	44	182	
	45	181	
	46	180	
	47	179	
	48	178	
	49	177	
	50	176	
	51	175	
	52	174	
	53	173	
	54	172	
	55	171	
	56	170	
	57	169	
	58	168	
	59	167	
	60	166	
	61	165	
	62	164	

		63	163
		64	162
		65	161

Anaerobic threshold	10K time	Marathon Heart rate
205	30	197
	31	196
	32	195
	33	194
	34	193
	35	192
	36	191
	37	190
	38	189
	39	188
	40	187
	41	186
	42	185
	43	184
	44	183
	45	182
	46	181
	47	180
	48	179
	49	178
	50	177
	51	176
	52	175
	53	174
	54	173
	55	172
	56	171

	57	170
	58	169
	59	168
	60	167
	61	166
	62	165
	63	164
	64	163
	65	162

Anaerobic threshold	10K time	Marathon Heart rate
206	30	198
	31	197
	32	196
	33	195
	34	194
	35	193
	36	192
	37	191
	38	190
	39	189
	40	188
	41	187
	42	186
	43	185
	44	184
	45	183
	46	182
	47	181
	48	180
	49	179
	50	178

		51	177
		52	176
		53	175
		54	174
		55	173
		56	172
		57	171
		58	170
		59	169
		60	168
		61	167
		62	166
		63	165
		64	164
		65	163

Anaerobic threshold	10K time	Marathon Heart rate
207	30	199
	31	198
	32	197
	33	196
	34	195
	35	194
	36	193
	37	192
	38	191
	39	190
	40	189
	41	188
	42	187
	43	186
	44	185

	45	184
	46	183
	47	182
	48	181
	49	180
	50	179
	51	178
	52	177
	53	176
	54	175
	55	174
	56	173
	57	172
	58	171
	59	170
	60	169
	61	168
	62	167
	63	166
	64	165
	65	164

Anaerobic threshold	10K time	Marathon Heart rate
208	30	200
	31	199
	32	198
	33	197
	34	196
	35	195
	36	194
	37	193
	38	192

	39	191
	40	190
	41	189
	42	188
	43	187
	44	186
	45	185
	46	184
	47	183
	48	182
	49	181
	50	180
	51	179
	52	178
	53	177
	54	176
	55	175
	56	174
	57	173
	58	172
	59	171
	60	170
	61	169
	62	168
	63	167
	64	166
	65	165

Anaerobic threshold	10K time	Marathon Heart rate
209	30	201
	31	200
	32	199

		33	198
		34	197
		35	196
		36	195
		37	194
		38	193
		39	192
		40	191
		41	190
		42	189
		43	188
		44	187
		45	186
		46	185
		47	184
		48	183
		49	182
		50	181
		51	180
		52	179
		53	178
		54	177
		55	176
		56	175
		57	174
		58	173
		59	172
		60	171
		61	170
		62	169
		63	168
		64	167
		65	166

Anaerobic threshold	10K time	Marathon Heart rate
210	30	202
	31	201
	32	200
	33	199
	34	198
	35	197
	36	196
	37	195
	38	194
	39	193
	40	192
	41	191
	42	190
	43	189
	44	188
	45	187
	46	186
	47	185
	48	184
	49	183
	50	182
	51	181
	52	180
	53	179
	54	178
	55	177
	56	176
	57	175
	58	174
	59	173
	60	172
	61	171

	62	170
	63	169
	64	168
	65	167

Chapter 7: Half Marathon schedule

Warning: training for a half marathon is harder than training for a full one if you train at the correct heart rate. That sounds crazy, but it is really true, because the half marathon takes less time. This allows you to run a relatively large number of kilometers or miles at a higher heart rate. I've added a column for runners that want to run a half marathon with a smile if a new personal best is not their main goal. The training sessions will be less intense, which is probably more enjoyable.

You will find your marathon heart rate at the end of this chapter. Each interval session is focused on making your body adjust to higher speeds. You will find your interval pace at the end of this chapter. Remember that the time in between the intervals is as long as the interval itself takes. So if you need to run a 400-meter interval in 1.38-1.32, you will also rest just as long. I advise you to run in zones 1 or 2 during the resting period instead of walking or standing still. This will make your body adjust to recovering during a run, which you might need if you started too fast during a race.

Week 1

Resting Heart rate	KM	Tempo for a PB	Tempo half marathon with a smile	Average pace	Average heart rate	Average cadence
	7	Half marathon Heart rate	Marathon heart rate			
	4	Interval (10x 400m)	Interval (10x 400m)			

Week 2

Resting Heart rate	KM	Tempo for a PB	Tempo half marathon with a smile	Average pace	Average heart rate	Average cadence
	7	Half marathon Heart rate	Marathon heart rate			
	5	Z1	Z1			
	4	Interval (4x 1000m)	Interval (4x 1000m)			
	7	Half marathon Heart rate	Marathon heart rate			

Week 3

Resting Heart rate	KM	Tempo for a PB	Tempo half marathon with a smile	Average pace	Average heart rate	Average cadence
	7	Half marathon Heart rate	Marathon heart rate			
	4	Z1	Z1			

| | 5 | Interval (2x 2000m +1000m) | Interval (2x 2000m +1000m) | | | |
| | 7 | Half marathon on Heart rate | Marathon heart rate | | | |

Week 4

Resting Heart rate	KM	Tempo for a PB	Tempo half marathon with a smile	Average pace	Average heart rate	Average cadence
	7	Half marathon on Heart rate	Marathon heart rate			
	4	Z1	Z1			
	5	Interval (12x 400m)	Interval (12x 400m)			
	8	AT	AT			

Week 5

Resting Heart rate	KM	Tempo for a PB	Tempo half marathon with a smile	Average pace	Average heart rate	Average cadence

	5	Z1	Z1			
	8	Half marathon Heart rate	Marathon heart rate			
	5	Interval (5x 1000m)	Interval (5x 1000m)			
	7	Half marathon Heart rate	Marathon heart rate			

Week 6

Resting Heart rate	KM	Tempo for a PB	Tempo half marathon with a smile	Average pace	Average heart rate	Average cadence
	8	Half marathon Heart rate	Marathon heart rate			
	5	Z1	Z1			
	5	Interval (2x 2000m +1000m)	Interval (2x 2000m +1000m)			
	8	Half marathon	Marathon heart rate			

		Heart rate				

Week 7

Resting Heart rate	KM	Tempo for a PB	Tempo half marathon with a smile	Average pace	Average heart rate	Average cadence
	8	Half marathon Heart rate	Marathon heart rate			
	5	Z1	Z1			
	5	Interval (12x 400m)	Interval (12x 400m)			
	10	AT	AT			

Week 8

Resting Heart rate	KM	Tempo for a PB	Tempo half marathon with a smile	Average pace	Average heart rate	Average cadence
	5	Z1	Z1			
	8	Half marathon Heart rate	Marathon heart rate			
	5	Interval (5x	Interval (5x			

| | | 1000m) | 1000m) | | | |
| | 8 | Half marathon Heart rate | Marathon heart rate | | | |

Week 9

Resting Heart rate	KM	Tempo for a PB	Tempo half marathon with a smile	Average pace	Average heart rate	Average cadence
	5	Z1	Z1			
	8	Half marathon Heart rate	Marathon heart rate			
	5	Interval (5x 1000m)	Interval (5x 1000m)			
	8	Half marathon Heart rate	Marathon heart rate			

Week 10

Resting Heart rate	KM	Tempo for a PB	Tempo half marathon with a smile	Average pace	Average heart rate	Average cadence

	6	Half marathon Heart rate	Marathon heart rate			
	5	Interval (2x 2000m +1000m)	Interval (2x 2000m +1000m)			
	5	Z1	Z1			
	10	AT	AT			

Week 11

Resting Heart rate	KM	Tempo for a PB	Tempo half marathon with a smile	Average pace	Average heart rate	Average cadence
	5	Z1	Z1			
	10	Half marathon Heart rate	Marathon heart rate			
	5	Interval (12x 400m)	Interval (12x 400m)			
	8	Half marathon Heart rate	Marathon heart rate			

Week 12

Resting Heart rate	KM	Tempo for a PB	Tempo half marathon with a smile	Average pace	Average heart rate	Average cadence
	6	Z1	Z1			
	10	Half marathon Heart rate	Marathon heart rate			
	5	Interval (5x 1000m)	Interval 5x 1000m			
	8	Half marathon Heart rate	Marathon heart rate			

Week 13 (toughest week)

Resting Heart rate	KM	Tempo for a PB	Tempo half marathon with a smile	Average pace	Average heart rate	Average cadence
	9	Half marathon Heart rate	Marathon heart rate			
	6	Interval (3x 2000m)	Interval (3x 2000m)			
	6	Z1	Z1			

	10	AT	AT			

Week 14

Resting Heart rate	KM	Tempo for a PB	Tempo half marathon with a smile	Average pace	Average heart rate	Average cadence
	6	Z1	Z1			
	9	Half marathon Heart rate	Marathon heart rate			
	5	Interval (5x 1000m)	Interval (5x 1000m)			

Week 15 (Tapering of training load for best performance)

Resting Heart rate	KM	Tempo for a PB	Tempo half marathon with a smile	Average pace	Average heart rate	Average cadence
	8	Half marathon Heart rate	Marathon heart rate			
	12 min	Half marathon tempo	Half marathon tempo			

	12 min	Half marathon tempo	Half marathon tempo			
	Half Marathon	Half marathon on Heart rate	Marathon heart rate			

Nutrition for the half marathon

The answer to how many calories do you need before a half marathon race depends on how fast you finish the race. Let's look at multiple finish time scenarios:

- If you finish under 1:30. You probably can get away with only 100 calories (25 grams of carbohydrates) followed by fuel on the race.
- If you finish under 2:00. You probably can get away with 200-300 calories (40-70 grams of carbohydrates) for a morning meal.
- If you finish under 2:30. You probably can eat 400-500 calories (80-110 grams of carbohydrates) plus fuel during the race.
- If you finish over 2:30. You probably can eat 500-600 calories (100-130 grams of carbohydrates) plus fuel during the race.

How much you need to drink and eat during the marathon to minimize dehydration depends on your body size and pace, the heat and humidity, and your sweat rate. The maximum amount you should drink while running is the amount your stomach can empty or the amount you've lost as sweat, whichever is less. You should drink enough during the marathon so you don't lose more than about 2 to 3 percent of your body weight during the race. Drinking more than you've lost increases the risk of hyponatremia.

Research has shown that most runners' stomachs can empty only about 180 to 210 ml (6 to 7 ounces) of fluid every 15 minutes during running, which represents about 720 to 840 ml (24 to 28 ounces) per hour. If you drink more than that, the extra fluid will slosh around in your stomach and not provide any additional benefit. You may need more or less than the average, so experiment with how much liquid and food your stomach can tolerate at a race pace. During running, it is very difficult to drink 200 ml of fluid at an aid station without stopping, and a 2007 study by Dr. Tim Noakes and colleagues found that most runners drink less than 480 ml (16 ounces) per hour when racing. But drinking and eating too little can certainly hamper your performance. It can easily cost you 30 minutes. So if you have trouble eating and drinking while running, I advise you to stop for a few seconds. This will take less time than the time you lose by not eating and drinking.

Moreover, I strongly advise you to practice drinking and eating during at least 2 training sessions. My stomach becomes upset after taking a gel, so instead, I take Gatorade as a drink and eat winegums. The advantage of Gatorade is that it also contains calories, so I still get enough calories, especially carbohydrates.

Time or distance	Nutrition
1 hour prior to the race	500 ml of liquid (17 ounces)
8K	Water cup (250ml) (8 ounces)

13K	Gel (100 calories)
15K	Water cup (250ml) (8 ounces)
17K	Gel (100 calories)

Interval Pace

10K time	Anaerobic threshold	2000m interval	1000m interval	400m interval	200m interval
30	3.09-3.04	7.00-6.30	3.23-3.08	1.15-1.09	34-31
31	3.15-3.10	7.12-6.42	3.29-3.14	1.17-1.11	35-32
32	3.21-3.16	7.24-6.54	3.35-3.20	1.19-1.13	36-33
33	3.27-3.22	7.36-7.06	3.41-3.26	1.22-1.16	37-33
34	3.33-3.28	7.48-7.18	3.47-3.32	1.24-1.18	38-33
35	3.39-3.34	8.00-7.30	3.53-3.38	1.26-1.20	38-34
36	3.45-3.40	8.12-7.42	3.59-3.44	1.29-1.23	39-35
37	3.51-3.46	8.24-7.54	4.05-3.50	1.31-1.25	40-36
38	3.57-3.52	8.36-8.06	4.11-3.56	1.33-1.27	41-36
39	4.03-3.58	8.48-8.18	4.17-4.02	1.36-1.30	42-37
40	4.09-4.04	9.00-8.30	4.23-4.08	1.38-1.32	43-38
41	4.15-4.10	9.12-8.42	4.29-4.14	1.40-1.34	44-48
42	4.21-.4.16	9.24-8.54	4.35-4.20	1.43-1.37	44-39
43	4.27-4.22	9.36-9.06	4.41-4.26	1.45-1.39	45-40
44	4.33-4.28	9.48-9.18	4.47-4.32	1.47-1.41	46-41
45	4.39-4.34	10.00-9.30	4.53-4.38	1.50-1.43	47-42
46	4.45-4.40	10.12-9.42	4.59-4.44	1.52-1.45	48-43
47	4.51-4.46	10.24-9.54	5.05-4.50	1.53-1.47	48-44
48	4.57-4.52	10.36-10.06	5.11-4.56	1.56-1.50	49-45

49	5.03-4.58	10.48-10.18	5.17-5.02	1.58-1.52	50-46
50	5.09-5.04	11.00-10.30	5.23-5.08	2.00-1.54	52-48
51	5.15-5.10	11.12-10.42	5.29-5.14	2.03-1.57	53-49
52	5.21-5.16	11.24-10.54	5.35-5.20	2.05-1.59	54-50
53	5.25-5.20	11.36-11.06	5.41-5.26	2.07-2.01	55-51
54	5.29-5.24	11.48-11.18	5.47-5.32	2.10-2.04	56-52
55	5.30	12.00-11.30	5.53-5.38	2.12-2.06	57-53
56	5.36	12.12-11.42	5.59-5.44	2.14-2.08	58-54
57	5.42	11.24-11.54	6.05-5.50	2.17-2.11	59-55
58	5.48	11.36-12.06	6.11-5.56	2.19-2.13	60-56
59	5.54	12.48-12.18	6.17-6.02	2.21-2.15	61-57
60	6.00	13.00-12.30	6.23-6.08	2.24-2.18	62-58
61	6.06	13.12-12.42	6.29-6.14	2.27-2.21	63-59
62	6.12	13.24-12.54	6.35-6.20	2.30-2.24	64-60
63	6.18	13.36-13.06	6.41-6.26	2.33-2.27	65-61
64	6.24	13.48-13.18	6.47-6.32	2.37-2.30	66-62
65	6.30	14.00-13.30	6.54-6.38	2.40-2.33	67-63

Half marathon Heart rate

Anaerobic threshold	10K time	Half marathon heart rate
139	30	144
	31	143
	32	142
	33	141
	34	140
	35	139
	36	138
	37	137
	38	136
	39	135

		40	134
		41	133
		42	132
		43	131
		44	130
		45	129
		46	128
		47	127
		48	126
		49	125
		50	124
		51	123
		52	122
		53	121
		54	120
		55	119
		56	118
		57	117
		58	116
		59	115
		60	114
		61	113
		62	112
		63	111
		64	110
		65	109

Anaerobic threshold	10K time	Half marathon heart rate
140		30	145
	31	144
	32	143
	33	142

	34	141
	35	140
	36	139
	37	138
	38	137
	39	136
	40	135
	41	134
	42	133
	43	132
	44	131
	45	130
	46	129
	47	128
	48	127
	49	126
	50	125
	51	124
	52	123
	53	122
	54	121
	55	120
	56	119
	57	118
	58	117
	59	116
	60	115
	61	114
	62	113
	63	112
	64	111
	65	110

Anaerobic threshold	10K time	Half marathon heart rate
141	30	146
	31	145
	32	144
	33	143
	34	142
	35	141
	36	140
	37	139
	38	138
	39	137
	40	136
	41	135
	42	134
	43	133
	44	132
	45	131
	46	130
	47	129
	48	128
	49	127
	50	126
	51	125
	52	124
	53	123
	54	122
	55	121
	56	120
	57	119
	58	118
	59	117
	60	116
	61	115

		62	114
		63	113
		64	112
		65	111

Anaerobic threshold	10K time	Half marathon heart rate
142	30	147
	31	146
	32	145
	33	144
	34	143
	35	142
	36	141
	37	140
	38	139
	39	138
	40	137
	41	136
	42	135
	43	134
	44	133
	45	132
	46	131
	47	130
	48	129
	49	128
	50	127
	51	126
	52	125
	53	124
	54	123
	55	122

		56	121
		57	120
		58	119
		59	118
		60	117
		61	116
		62	115
		63	114
		64	113
		65	112

Anaerobic threshold	10K time	Half marathon heart rate
143	30	148
	31	147
	32	146
	33	145
	34	144
	35	143
	36	142
	37	141
	38	140
	39	139
	40	138
	41	137
	42	136
	43	135
	44	134
	45	133
	46	132
	47	131
	48	130
	49	129

		50	128
		51	127
		52	126
		53	125
		54	124
		55	123
		56	122
		57	121
		58	120
		59	119
		60	118
		61	117
		62	116
		63	115
		64	114
		65	113

Anaerobic threshold	10K time	Half marathon heart rate
144	30	149
	31	148
	32	147
	33	146
	34	145
	35	144
	36	143
	37	142
	38	141
	39	140
	40	139
	41	138
	42	137
	43	136

	44	135
	45	134
	46	133
	47	132
	48	131
	49	130
	50	129
	51	128
	52	127
	53	126
	54	125
	55	124
	56	123
	57	122
	58	121
	59	120
	60	119
	61	118
	62	117
	63	116
	64	115
	65	114

Anaerobic threshold	10K time	Half marathon heart rate
145	30	150
	31	149
	32	148
	33	147
	34	146
	35	145
	36	144
	37	143

	38	142
	39	141
	40	140
	41	139
	42	138
	43	137
	44	136
	45	135
	46	134
	47	133
	48	132
	49	131
	50	130
	51	129
	52	128
	53	127
	54	126
	55	125
	56	124
	57	123
	58	122
	59	121
	60	120
	61	119
	62	118
	63	117
	64	116
	65	115

Anaerobic threshold	10K time	Half marathon heart rate
146	30	151
	31	150

	32	149
	33	148
	34	147
	35	146
	36	145
	37	144
	38	143
	39	142
	40	141
	41	140
	42	139
	43	138
	44	137
	45	136
	46	135
	47	134
	48	133
	49	132
	50	131
	51	130
	52	129
	53	128
	54	127
	55	126
	56	125
	57	124
	58	123
	59	122
	60	121
	61	120
	62	119
	63	118
	64	117

		65	116

Anaerobic threshold	10K time	Half marathon heart rate
147	30	152
	31	151
	32	150
	33	149
	34	148
	35	147
	36	146
	37	145
	38	144
	39	143
	40	142
	41	141
	42	140
	43	139
	44	138
	45	137
	46	136
	47	135
	48	134
	49	133
	50	132
	51	131
	52	130
	53	129
	54	128
	55	127
	56	126
	57	125
	58	124

	59	123
	60	122
	61	121
	62	120
	63	119
	64	118
	65	117

Anaerobic threshold	10K time	Half marathon heart rate
148	30	153
	31	152
	32	151
	33	150
	34	149
	35	148
	36	147
	37	146
	38	145
	39	144
	40	143
	41	142
	42	141
	43	140
	44	139
	45	138
	46	137
	47	136
	48	135
	49	134
	50	133
	51	132
	52	131

	53	130
	54	129
	55	128
	56	127
	57	126
	58	125
	59	124
	60	123
	61	122
	62	121
	63	120
	64	119
	65	118

Anaerobic threshold	10K time	Half marathon heart rate
149	30	154
	31	153
	32	152
	33	151
	34	150
	35	149
	36	148
	37	147
	38	146
	39	145
	40	144
	41	143
	42	142
	43	141
	44	140
	45	139
	46	138

	47	137
	48	136
	49	135
	50	134
	51	133
	52	132
	53	131
	54	130
	55	129
	56	128
	57	127
	58	126
	59	125
	60	124
	61	123
	62	122
	63	121
	64	120
	65	119

Anaerobic threshold	10K time	Half marathon heart rate
150	30	155
	31	154
	32	153
	33	152
	34	151
	35	150
	36	149
	37	148
	38	147
	39	146
	40	145

	41	144
	42	143
	43	142
	44	141
	45	140
	46	139
	47	138
	48	137
	49	136
	50	135
	51	134
	52	133
	53	132
	54	131
	55	130
	56	129
	57	128
	58	127
	59	126
	60	125
	61	124
	62	123
	63	122
	64	121
	65	120

Anaerobic threshold	10K time	Half marathon heart rate
151	30	156
	31	155
	32	154
	33	153
	34	152

	35	151
	36	150
	37	149
	38	148
	39	147
	40	146
	41	145
	42	144
	43	143
	44	142
	45	141
	46	140
	47	139
	48	138
	49	137
	50	136
	51	135
	52	134
	53	133
	54	132
	55	131
	56	130
	57	129
	58	128
	59	127
	60	126
	61	125
	62	124
	63	123
	64	122
	65	121

| Anaerobic | 10K time | Half marathon |

threshold		heart rate
152	30	157
	31	156
	32	155
	33	154
	34	153
	35	152
	36	151
	37	150
	38	149
	39	148
	40	147
	41	146
	42	145
	43	144
	44	143
	45	142
	46	141
	47	140
	48	139
	49	138
	50	137
	51	136
	52	135
	53	134
	54	133
	55	132
	56	131
	57	130
	58	129
	59	128
	60	127
	61	126
	62	125

	63	124
	64	123
	65	122

Anaerobic threshold	10K time	Half marathon heart rate
153	30	158
	31	157
	32	156
	33	155
	34	154
	35	153
	36	152
	37	151
	38	150
	39	149
	40	148
	41	147
	42	146
	43	145
	44	144
	45	143
	46	142
	47	141
	48	140
	49	139
	50	138
	51	137
	52	136
	53	135
	54	134
	55	133
	56	132

	57	131
	58	130
	59	129
	60	128
	61	127
	62	126
	63	125
	64	124
	65	123

Anaerobic threshold	10K time	Half marathon heart rate
154	30	159
	31	158
	32	157
	33	156
	34	155
	35	154
	36	153
	37	152
	38	151
	39	150
	40	149
	41	148
	42	147
	43	146
	44	145
	45	144
	46	143
	47	142
	48	141
	49	140
	50	139

	51	138
	52	137
	53	136
	54	135
	55	134
	56	133
	57	132
	58	131
	59	130
	60	129
	61	128
	62	127
	63	126
	64	125
	65	124

Anaerobic threshold	10K time	Half marathon heart rate
155	30	160
	31	159
	32	158
	33	157
	34	156
	35	155
	36	154
	37	153
	38	152
	39	151
	40	150
	41	149
	42	148
	43	147
	44	146

		45	145
		46	144
		47	143
		48	142
		49	141
		50	140
		51	139
		52	138
		53	137
		54	136
		55	135
		56	134
		57	133
		58	132
		59	131
		60	130
		61	129
		62	128
		63	127
		64	126
		65	125

Anaerobic threshold	10K time	Half marathon heart rate
156	30	161
	31	160
	32	159
	33	158
	34	157
	35	156
	36	155
	37	154
	38	153

	39	152
	40	151
	41	150
	42	149
	43	148
	44	147
	45	146
	46	145
	47	144
	48	143
	49	142
	50	141
	51	140
	52	139
	53	138
	54	137
	55	136
	56	135
	57	134
	58	133
	59	132
	60	131
	61	130
	62	129
	63	128
	64	127
	65	126

Anaerobic threshold	10K time	Half marathon heart rate
157	30	162
	31	161
	32	160

		33	159
		34	158
		35	157
		36	156
		37	155
		38	154
		39	153
		40	152
		41	151
		42	150
		43	149
		44	148
		45	147
		46	146
		47	145
		48	144
		49	143
		50	142
		51	141
		52	140
		53	139
		54	138
		55	137
		56	136
		57	135
		58	134
		59	133
		60	132
		61	131
		62	130
		63	129
		64	128
		65	127

Anaerobic threshold	10K time	Half marathon heart rate
158	30	163
	31	162
	32	161
	33	160
	34	159
	35	158
	36	157
	37	156
	38	155
	39	154
	40	153
	41	152
	42	151
	43	150
	44	149
	45	148
	46	147
	47	146
	48	145
	49	144
	50	143
	51	142
	52	141
	53	140
	54	139
	55	138
	56	137
	57	136
	58	135
	59	134
	60	133
	61	132

	62	131
	63	130
	64	129
	65	128

Anaerobic threshold	10K time	Half marathon heart rate
159	30	164
	31	163
	32	162
	33	161
	34	160
	35	159
	36	158
	37	157
	38	156
	39	155
	40	154
	41	153
	42	152
	43	151
	44	150
	45	149
	46	148
	47	147
	48	146
	49	145
	50	144
	51	143
	52	142
	53	141
	54	140
	55	139

	56	138
	57	137
	58	136
	59	135
	60	134
	61	133
	62	132
	63	131
	64	130
	65	129

Anaerobic threshold	10K time	Half marathon heart rate
160	30	165
	31	164
	32	163
	33	162
	34	161
	35	160
	36	159
	37	158
	38	157
	39	156
	40	155
	41	154
	42	153
	43	152
	44	151
	45	150
	46	149
	47	148
	48	147
	49	146

		50	145
		51	144
		52	143
		53	142
		54	141
		55	140
		56	139
		57	138
		58	137
		59	136
		60	135
		61	134
		62	133
		63	132
		64	131
		65	130

Anaerobic threshold	10K time	Half marathon heart rate
161	30	166
	31	165
	32	164
	33	163
	34	162
	35	161
	36	160
	37	159
	38	158
	39	157
	40	156
	41	155
	42	154
	43	153

		44	152
		45	151
		46	150
		47	149
		48	148
		49	147
		50	146
		51	145
		52	144
		53	143
		54	142
		55	141
		56	140
		57	139
		58	138
		59	137
		60	136
		61	135
		62	134
		63	133
		64	132
		65	131

Anaerobic threshold	10K time	Half marathon heart rate
162	30	167
	31	166
	32	165
	33	164
	34	163
	35	162
	36	161
	37	160

		38	159
		39	158
		40	157
		41	156
		42	155
		43	154
		44	153
		45	152
		46	151
		47	150
		48	149
		49	148
		50	147
		51	146
		52	145
		53	144
		54	143
		55	142
		56	141
		57	140
		58	139
		59	138
		60	137
		61	136
		62	135
		63	134
		64	133
		65	132

Anaerobic threshold	10K time		Half marathon heart rate
163		30	168
		31	167

		32	166
		33	165
		34	164
		35	163
		36	162
		37	161
		38	160
		39	159
		40	158
		41	157
		42	156
		43	155
		44	154
		45	153
		46	152
		47	151
		48	150
		49	149
		50	148
		51	147
		52	146
		53	145
		54	144
		55	143
		56	142
		57	141
		58	140
		59	139
		60	138
		61	137
		62	136
		63	135
		64	134

	65	133

Anaerobic threshold	10K time	Half marathon heart rate
164	30	169
	31	168
	32	167
	33	166
	34	165
	35	164
	36	163
	37	162
	38	161
	39	160
	40	159
	41	158
	42	157
	43	156
	44	155
	45	154
	46	153
	47	152
	48	151
	49	150
	50	149
	51	148
	52	147
	53	146
	54	145
	55	144
	56	143
	57	142
	58	141

	59	140
	60	139
	61	138
	62	137
	63	136
	64	135
	65	134

Anaerobic threshold	10K time	Half marathon heart rate
165	30	170
	31	169
	32	168
	33	167
	34	166
	35	165
	36	164
	37	163
	38	162
	39	161
	40	160
	41	159
	42	158
	43	157
	44	156
	45	155
	46	154
	47	153
	48	152
	49	151
	50	150
	51	149
	52	148

	53	147
	54	146
	55	145
	56	144
	57	143
	58	142
	59	141
	60	140
	61	139
	62	138
	63	137
	64	136
	65	135

Anaerobic threshold	10K time	Half marathon heart rate
166	30	171
	31	170
	32	169
	33	168
	34	167
	35	166
	36	165
	37	164
	38	163
	39	162
	40	161
	41	160
	42	159
	43	158
	44	157
	45	156
	46	155

	47	154
	48	153
	49	152
	50	151
	51	150
	52	149
	53	148
	54	147
	55	146
	56	145
	57	144
	58	143
	59	142
	60	141
	61	140
	62	139
	63	138
	64	137
	65	136

Anaerobic threshold	10K time	Half marathon heart rate
167	30	172
	31	171
	32	170
	33	169
	34	168
	35	167
	36	166
	37	165
	38	164
	39	163
	40	162

		41	161
		42	160
		43	159
		44	158
		45	157
		46	156
		47	155
		48	154
		49	153
		50	152
		51	151
		52	150
		53	149
		54	148
		55	147
		56	146
		57	145
		58	144
		59	143
		60	142
		61	141
		62	140
		63	139
		64	138
		65	137

Anaerobic threshold	10K time	Half marathon heart rate
168	30	173
	31	172
	32	171
	33	170
	34	169

		35	168
		36	167
		37	166
		38	165
		39	164
		40	163
		41	162
		42	161
		43	160
		44	159
		45	158
		46	157
		47	156
		48	155
		49	154
		50	153
		51	152
		52	151
		53	150
		54	149
		55	148
		56	147
		57	146
		58	145
		59	144
		60	143
		61	142
		62	141
		63	140
		64	139
		65	138

Anaerobic	10K time	Half marathon

threshold		heart rate
169	30	174
	31	173
	32	172
	33	171
	34	170
	35	169
	36	168
	37	167
	38	166
	39	165
	40	164
	41	163
	42	162
	43	161
	44	160
	45	159
	46	158
	47	157
	48	156
	49	155
	50	154
	51	153
	52	152
	53	151
	54	150
	55	149
	56	148
	57	147
	58	146
	59	145
	60	144
	61	143
	62	142

	63	141
	64	140
	65	139

Anaerobic threshold	10K time	Half marathon heart rate
170	30	175
	31	174
	32	173
	33	172
	34	171
	35	170
	36	169
	37	168
	38	167
	39	166
	40	165
	41	164
	42	163
	43	162
	44	161
	45	160
	46	159
	47	158
	48	157
	49	156
	50	155
	51	154
	52	153
	53	152
	54	151
	55	150
	56	149

	57	148
	58	147
	59	146
	60	145
	61	144
	62	143
	63	142
	64	141
	65	140

Anaerobic threshold	10K time	Half marathon heart rate
171	30	176
	31	175
	32	174
	33	173
	34	172
	35	171
	36	170
	37	169
	38	168
	39	167
	40	166
	41	165
	42	164
	43	163
	44	162
	45	161
	46	160
	47	159
	48	158
	49	157
	50	156

	51	155
	52	154
	53	153
	54	152
	55	151
	56	150
	57	149
	58	148
	59	147
	60	146
	61	145
	62	144
	63	143
	64	142
	65	141

Anaerobic threshold	10K time	Half marathon heart rate
172	30	177
	31	176
	32	175
	33	174
	34	173
	35	172
	36	171
	37	170
	38	169
	39	168
	40	167
	41	166
	42	165
	43	164
	44	163

	45	162
	46	161
	47	160
	48	159
	49	158
	50	157
	51	156
	52	155
	53	154
	54	153
	55	152
	56	151
	57	150
	58	149
	59	148
	60	147
	61	146
	62	145
	63	144
	64	143
	65	142

Anaerobic threshold	10K time	Half marathon heart rate
173	30	178
	31	177
	32	176
	33	175
	34	174
	35	173
	36	172
	37	171
	38	170

		39	169
		40	168
		41	167
		42	166
		43	165
		44	164
		45	163
		46	162
		47	161
		48	160
		49	159
		50	158
		51	157
		52	156
		53	155
		54	154
		55	153
		56	152
		57	151
		58	150
		59	149
		60	148
		61	147
		62	146
		63	145
		64	144
		65	143

Anaerobic threshold	10K time	Half marathon heart rate
174	30	179
	31	178
	32	177

		33	176
		34	175
		35	174
		36	173
		37	172
		38	171
		39	170
		40	169
		41	168
		42	167
		43	166
		44	165
		45	164
		46	163
		47	162
		48	161
		49	160
		50	159
		51	158
		52	157
		53	156
		54	155
		55	154
		56	153
		57	152
		58	151
		59	150
		60	149
		61	148
		62	147
		63	146
		64	145
		65	144

Anaerobic threshold	10K time	Half marathon heart rate
175	30	180
	31	179
	32	178
	33	177
	34	176
	35	175
	36	174
	37	173
	38	172
	39	171
	40	170
	41	169
	42	168
	43	167
	44	166
	45	165
	46	164
	47	163
	48	162
	49	161
	50	160
	51	159
	52	158
	53	157
	54	156
	55	155
	56	154
	57	153
	58	152
	59	151
	60	150
	61	149

	62	148
	63	147
	64	146
	65	145

Anaerobic threshold	10K time	Half marathon heart rate
176	30	181
	31	180
	32	179
	33	178
	34	177
	35	176
	36	175
	37	174
	38	173
	39	172
	40	171
	41	170
	42	169
	43	168
	44	167
	45	166
	46	165
	47	164
	48	163
	49	162
	50	161
	51	160
	52	159
	53	158
	54	157
	55	156

		56	155
		57	154
		58	153
		59	152
		60	151
		61	150
		62	149
		63	148
		64	147
		65	146

Anaerobic threshold	10K time	Half marathon heart rate
177	30	182
	31	181
	32	180
	33	179
	34	178
	35	177
	36	176
	37	175
	38	174
	39	173
	40	172
	41	171
	42	170
	43	169
	44	168
	45	167
	46	166
	47	165
	48	164
	49	163

	50	162
	51	161
	52	160
	53	159
	54	158
	55	157
	56	156
	57	155
	58	154
	59	153
	60	152
	61	151
	62	150
	63	149
	64	148
	65	147

Anaerobic threshold	10K time	Half marathon heart rate
178	30	183
	31	182
	32	181
	33	180
	34	179
	35	178
	36	177
	37	176
	38	175
	39	174
	40	173
	41	172
	42	171
	43	170

		44	169
		45	168
		46	167
		47	166
		48	165
		49	164
		50	163
		51	162
		52	161
		53	160
		54	159
		55	158
		56	157
		57	156
		58	155
		59	154
		60	153
		61	152
		62	151
		63	150
		64	149
		65	148

Anaerobic threshold	10K time	Half marathon heart rate
179	30	184
	31	183
	32	182
	33	181
	34	180
	35	179
	36	178
	37	177

		38	176
		39	175
		40	174
		41	173
		42	172
		43	171
		44	170
		45	169
		46	168
		47	167
		48	166
		49	165
		50	164
		51	163
		52	162
		53	161
		54	160
		55	159
		56	158
		57	157
		58	156
		59	155
		60	154
		61	153
		62	152
		63	151
		64	150
		65	149

Anaerobic threshold	10K time	Half marathon heart rate
180	30	185
	31	184

		32	183
		33	182
		34	181
		35	180
		36	179
		37	178
		38	177
		39	176
		40	175
		41	174
		42	173
		43	172
		44	171
		45	170
		46	169
		47	168
		48	167
		49	166
		50	165
		51	164
		52	163
		53	162
		54	161
		55	160
		56	159
		57	158
		58	157
		59	156
		60	155
		61	154
		62	153
		63	152
		64	151

		65	150

Anaerobic threshold	10K time	Half marathon heart rate
181	30	186
	31	185
	32	184
	33	183
	34	182
	35	181
	36	180
	37	179
	38	178
	39	177
	40	176
	41	175
	42	174
	43	173
	44	172
	45	171
	46	170
	47	169
	48	168
	49	167
	50	166
	51	165
	52	164
	53	163
	54	162
	55	161
	56	160
	57	159
	58	158

		59	157
		60	156
		61	155
		62	154
		63	153
		64	152
		65	151

Anaerobic threshold	10K time	Half marathon heart rate
182	30	187
	31	186
	32	185
	33	184
	34	183
	35	182
	36	181
	37	180
	38	179
	39	178
	40	177
	41	176
	42	175
	43	174
	44	173
	45	172
	46	171
	47	170
	48	169
	49	168
	50	167
	51	166
	52	165

	53	164
	54	163
	55	162
	56	161
	57	160
	58	159
	59	158
	60	157
	61	156
	62	155
	63	154
	64	153
	65	152

Anaerobic threshold	10K time	Half marathon heart rate
183	30	188
	31	187
	32	186
	33	185
	34	184
	35	183
	36	182
	37	181
	38	180
	39	179
	40	178
	41	177
	42	176
	43	175
	44	174
	45	173
	46	172

		47	171
		48	170
		49	169
		50	168
		51	167
		52	166
		53	165
		54	164
		55	163
		56	162
		57	161
		58	160
		59	159
		60	158
		61	157
		62	156
		63	155
		64	154
		65	153

Anaerobic threshold	10K time	Half marathon heart rate
184	30	189
	31	188
	32	187
	33	186
	34	185
	35	184
	36	183
	37	182
	38	181
	39	180
	40	179

	41	178
	42	177
	43	176
	44	175
	45	174
	46	173
	47	172
	48	171
	49	170
	50	169
	51	168
	52	167
	53	166
	54	165
	55	164
	56	163
	57	162
	58	161
	59	160
	60	159
	61	158
	62	157
	63	156
	64	155
	65	154

Anaerobic threshold	10K time	Half marathon heart rate
185	30	190
	31	189
	32	188
	33	187
	34	186

		35	185
		36	184
		37	183
		38	182
		39	181
		40	180
		41	179
		42	178
		43	177
		44	176
		45	175
		46	174
		47	173
		48	172
		49	171
		50	170
		51	169
		52	168
		53	167
		54	166
		55	165
		56	164
		57	163
		58	162
		59	161
		60	160
		61	159
		62	158
		63	157
		64	156
		65	155

Anaerobic	10K time	Half marathon

threshold			heart rate
186		30	191
		31	190
		32	189
		33	188
		34	187
		35	186
		36	185
		37	184
		38	183
		39	182
		40	181
		41	180
		42	179
		43	178
		44	177
		45	176
		46	175
		47	174
		48	173
		49	172
		50	171
		51	170
		52	169
		53	168
		54	167
		55	166
		56	165
		57	164
		58	163
		59	162
		60	161
		61	160
		62	159

	63	158
	64	157
	65	156

Anaerobic threshold	10K time	Half marathon heart rate
187	30	192
	31	191
	32	190
	33	189
	34	188
	35	187
	36	186
	37	185
	38	184
	39	183
	40	182
	41	181
	42	180
	43	179
	44	178
	45	177
	46	176
	47	175
	48	174
	49	173
	50	172
	51	171
	52	170
	53	169
	54	168
	55	167
	56	166

		57	165
		58	164
		59	163
		60	162
		61	161
		62	160
		63	159
		64	158
		65	157

Anaerobic threshold	10K time	Half marathon heart rate
188	30	193
	31	192
	32	191
	33	190
	34	189
	35	188
	36	187
	37	186
	38	185
	39	184
	40	183
	41	182
	42	181
	43	180
	44	179
	45	178
	46	177
	47	176
	48	175
	49	174
	50	173

	51	172
	52	171
	53	170
	54	169
	55	168
	56	167
	57	166
	58	165
	59	164
	60	163
	61	162
	62	161
	63	160
	64	159
	65	158

Anaerobic threshold	10K time	Half marathon heart rate
189	30	194
	31	193
	32	192
	33	191
	34	190
	35	189
	36	188
	37	187
	38	186
	39	185
	40	184
	41	183
	42	182
	43	181
	44	180

	45	179
	46	178
	47	177
	48	176
	49	175
	50	174
	51	173
	52	172
	53	171
	54	170
	55	169
	56	168
	57	167
	58	166
	59	165
	60	164
	61	163
	62	162
	63	161
	64	160
	65	159

Anaerobic threshold	10K time	Half marathon heart rate
190	30	195
	31	194
	32	193
	33	192
	34	191
	35	190
	36	189
	37	188
	38	187

	39	186
	40	185
	41	184
	42	183
	43	182
	44	181
	45	180
	46	179
	47	178
	48	177
	49	176
	50	175
	51	174
	52	173
	53	172
	54	171
	55	170
	56	169
	57	168
	58	167
	59	166
	60	165
	61	164
	62	163
	63	162
	64	161
	65	160

Anaerobic threshold	10K time	Half marathon heart rate
191	30	196
	31	195
	32	194

	33	193
	34	192
	35	191
	36	190
	37	189
	38	188
	39	187
	40	186
	41	185
	42	184
	43	183
	44	182
	45	181
	46	180
	47	179
	48	178
	49	177
	50	176
	51	175
	52	174
	53	173
	54	172
	55	171
	56	170
	57	169
	58	168
	59	167
	60	166
	61	165
	62	164
	63	163
	64	162
	65	161

Anaerobic threshold	10K time	Half marathon heart rate
192	30	197
	31	196
	32	195
	33	194
	34	193
	35	192
	36	191
	37	190
	38	189
	39	188
	40	187
	41	186
	42	185
	43	184
	44	183
	45	182
	46	181
	47	180
	48	179
	49	178
	50	177
	51	176
	52	175
	53	174
	54	173
	55	172
	56	171
	57	170
	58	169
	59	168
	60	167
	61	166

		62	165
		63	164
		64	163
		65	162

Anaerobic threshold	10K time	Half marathon heart rate
193	30	198
	31	197
	32	196
	33	195
	34	194
	35	193
	36	192
	37	191
	38	190
	39	189
	40	188
	41	187
	42	186
	43	185
	44	184
	45	183
	46	182
	47	181
	48	180
	49	179
	50	178
	51	177
	52	176
	53	175
	54	174
	55	173

	56	172
	57	171
	58	170
	59	169
	60	168
	61	167
	62	166
	63	165
	64	164
	65	163

Anaerobic threshold	10K time	Half marathon heart rate
191	30	199
	31	198
	32	197
	33	196
	34	195
	35	194
	36	193
	37	192
	38	191
	39	190
	40	189
	41	188
	42	187
	43	186
	44	185
	45	184
	46	183
	47	182
	48	181
	49	180

	50	179
	51	178
	52	177
	53	176
	54	175
	55	174
	56	173
	57	172
	58	171
	59	170
	60	169
	61	168
	62	167
	63	166
	64	165
	65	164

Anaerobic threshold	10K time	Half marathon heart rate
195	30	200
	31	199
	32	198
	33	197
	34	196
	35	195
	36	194
	37	193
	38	192
	39	191
	40	190
	41	189
	42	188
	43	187

		44	186
		45	185
		46	184
		47	183
		48	182
		49	181
		50	180
		51	179
		52	178
		53	177
		54	176
		55	175
		56	174
		57	173
		58	172
		59	171
		60	170
		61	169
		62	168
		63	167
		64	166
		65	165

Anaerobic threshold	10K time	Half marathon heart rate
196	30	201
	31	200
	32	199
	33	198
	34	197
	35	196
	36	195
	37	194

	38	193
	39	192
	40	191
	41	190
	42	189
	43	188
	44	187
	45	186
	46	185
	47	184
	48	183
	49	182
	50	181
	51	180
	52	179
	53	178
	54	177
	55	176
	56	175
	57	174
	58	173
	59	172
	60	171
	61	170
	62	169
	63	168
	64	167
	65	166

Anaerobic threshold	10K time	Half marathon heart rate
197	30	202
	31	201

		32	200
		33	199
		34	198
		35	197
		36	196
		37	195
		38	194
		39	193
		40	192
		41	191
		42	190
		43	189
		44	188
		45	187
		46	186
		47	185
		48	184
		49	183
		50	182
		51	181
		52	180
		53	179
		54	178
		55	177
		56	176
		57	175
		58	174
		59	173
		60	172
		61	171
		62	170
		63	169
		64	168

		65	167

Anaerobic threshold	10K time	Half marathon heart rate
198	30	203
	31	202
	32	201
	33	200
	34	199
	35	198
	36	197
	37	196
	38	195
	39	194
	40	193
	41	192
	42	191
	43	190
	44	189
	45	188
	46	187
	47	186
	48	185
	49	184
	50	183
	51	182
	52	181
	53	180
	54	179
	55	178
	56	177
	57	176
	58	175

	59	174
	60	173
	61	172
	62	171
	63	170
	64	169
	65	168

Anaerobic threshold	10K time	Half marathon heart rate
199	30	204
	31	203
	32	202
	33	201
	34	200
	35	199
	36	198
	37	197
	38	196
	39	195
	40	194
	41	193
	42	192
	43	191
	44	190
	45	189
	46	188
	47	187
	48	186
	49	185
	50	184
	51	183
	52	182

		53	181
		54	180
		55	179
		56	178
		57	177
		58	176
		59	175
		60	174
		61	173
		62	172
		63	171
		64	170
		65	169

Anaerobic threshold	10K time	Half marathon heart rate
200	30	205
	31	204
	32	203
	33	202
	34	201
	35	200
	36	199
	37	198
	38	197
	39	196
	40	195
	41	194
	42	193
	43	192
	44	191
	45	190
	46	189

	47	188
	48	187
	49	186
	50	185
	51	184
	52	183
	53	182
	54	181
	55	180
	56	179
	57	178
	58	177
	59	176
	60	175
	61	174
	62	173
	63	172
	64	171
	65	170

Anaerobic threshold	10K time	Half marathon heart rate
201	30	206
	31	205
	32	204
	33	203
	34	202
	35	201
	36	200
	37	199
	38	198
	39	197
	40	196

		41	195
		42	194
		43	193
		44	192
		45	191
		46	190
		47	189
		48	188
		49	187
		50	186
		51	185
		52	184
		53	183
		54	182
		55	181
		56	180
		57	179
		58	178
		59	177
		60	176
		61	175
		62	174
		63	173
		64	172
		65	171

Anaerobic threshold	10K time	Half marathon heart rate
202	30	207
	31	206
	32	205
	33	204
	34	203

	35	202
	36	201
	37	200
	38	199
	39	198
	40	197
	41	196
	42	195
	43	194
	44	193
	45	192
	46	191
	47	190
	48	189
	49	188
	50	187
	51	186
	52	185
	53	184
	54	183
	55	182
	56	181
	57	180
	58	179
	59	178
	60	177
	61	176
	62	175
	63	174
	64	173
	65	172

Anaerobic	10K time	Half marathon

threshold		heart rate
203	30	208
	31	207
	32	206
	33	205
	34	204
	35	203
	36	202
	37	201
	38	200
	39	199
	40	198
	41	197
	42	196
	43	195
	44	194
	45	193
	46	192
	47	191
	48	190
	49	189
	50	188
	51	187
	52	186
	53	185
	54	184
	55	183
	56	182
	57	181
	58	180
	59	179
	60	178
	61	177
	62	176

		63	175
		64	174
		65	173

Anaerobic threshold	10K time	Half marathon heart rate
204	30	209
	31	208
	32	207
	33	206
	34	205
	35	204
	36	203
	37	202
	38	201
	39	200
	40	199
	41	198
	42	197
	43	196
	44	195
	45	194
	46	193
	47	192
	48	191
	49	190
	50	189
	51	188
	52	187
	53	186
	54	185
	55	184
	56	183

	57	182
	58	181
	59	180
	60	179
	61	178
	62	177
	63	176
	64	175
	65	174

Anaerobic threshold	10K time	Half marathon heart rate
205	30	210
	31	209
	32	208
	33	207
	34	206
	35	205
	36	204
	37	203
	38	202
	39	201
	40	200
	41	199
	42	198
	43	197
	44	196
	45	195
	46	194
	47	193
	48	192
	49	191
	50	190

		51	189
		52	188
		53	187
		54	186
		55	185
		56	184
		57	183
		58	182
		59	181
		60	180
		61	179
		62	178
		63	177
		64	176
		65	175

Anaerobic threshold	10K time	Half marathon heart rate
206	30	211
	31	210
	32	209
	33	208
	34	207
	35	206
	36	205
	37	204
	38	203
	39	202
	40	201
	41	200
	42	199
	43	198
	44	197

	45	196
	46	195
	47	194
	48	193
	49	192
	50	191
	51	190
	52	189
	53	188
	54	187
	55	186
	56	185
	57	184
	58	183
	59	182
	60	181
	61	180
	62	179
	63	178
	64	177
	65	176

Anaerobic threshold	10K time	Half marathon heart rate
207	30	212
	31	211
	32	210
	33	209
	34	208
	35	207
	36	206
	37	205
	38	204

		39	203
		40	202
		41	201
		42	200
		43	199
		44	198
		45	197
		46	196
		47	195
		48	194
		49	193
		50	192
		51	191
		52	190
		53	189
		54	188
		55	187
		56	186
		57	185
		58	184
		59	183
		60	182
		61	181
		62	180
		63	179
		64	178
		65	177

Anaerobic threshold	10K time	Half marathon heart rate
208	30	213
	31	212
	32	211

		33	210
		34	209
		35	208
		36	207
		37	206
		38	205
		39	204
		40	203
		41	202
		42	201
		43	200
		44	199
		45	198
		46	197
		47	196
		48	195
		49	194
		50	193
		51	192
		52	191
		53	190
		54	189
		55	188
		56	187
		57	186
		58	185
		59	184
		60	183
		61	182
		62	181
		63	180
		64	179
		65	178

Anaerobic threshold	10K time	Half marathon heart rate
209	30	214
	31	213
	32	212
	33	211
	34	210
	35	209
	36	208
	37	207
	38	206
	39	205
	40	204
	41	203
	42	202
	43	201
	44	200
	45	199
	46	198
	47	197
	48	196
	49	195
	50	194
	51	193
	52	192
	53	191
	54	190
	55	189
	56	188
	57	187
	58	186
	59	185
	60	184
	61	183

		62	182
		63	181
		64	180
		65	179

Anaerobic threshold	10K time	Half marathon heart rate
210	30	215
	31	214
	32	213
	33	212
	34	211
	35	210
	36	209
	37	208
	38	207
	39	206
	40	205
	41	204
	42	203
	43	202
	44	201
	45	200
	46	199
	47	198
	48	197
	49	196
	50	195
	51	194
	52	193
	53	192
	54	191
	55	190

	56	189
	57	188
	58	187
	59	186
	60	185
	61	184
	62	183
	63	182
	64	181
	65	180

Chapter 8: 10K schedule

Each interval session is focused on making your body adjust to higher speeds. You will find your interval pace at the end of this chapter. Remember that the time in between the intervals is as long as the interval itself takes. So if you need to run a 400-meter interval in 1.38-1.32, you will also rest just as long. I advise you to run in zones 1 or 2 during the resting period instead of walking or standing still. This will help your body adjust to being able to recover during a run, which you might need if you started running too fast during a race.

Week 1

Resting Heart rate	KM	Tempo 10K with a smile 10K with a smile	Heart rate zone for a PB	Average pace	Average heart rate	Average cadence
	4	Z3	Anaerobic threshold			
	2	5x 400m	5x 400m			
	3	Z1	Z1			

Week 2

Resting Heart rate	KM	Tempo 10K with a smile	Heart rate zone for a PB	Average pace	Average heart rate	Average cadence
	5	Z3	Anaerobic threshold			

| | 3 | 8x 400m | 8x 400m | | | |
| | 4 | Z1 | Z1 | | | |

Week 3

Resting Heart rate	KM	Tempo 10K with a smile	Heart rate zone for a PB	Average pace	Average heart rate	Average cadence
	5	Z3	Anaerobic threshold			
	3	8x 400m	8x 400m			
	4	Z1	Z1			

Week 4

Resting Heart rate	KM	Tempo 10K with a smile	Heart rate zone for a PB	Average pace	Average heart rate	Average cadence
	5	AT	AT			
	3	Z1	Z1			
	4	4x 1000m	4x 1000m			

Week 5

Resting Heart rate	KM	Tempo 10K with a smile	Heart rate zone for a PB	Average pace	Average heart rate	Average cadence
	6	Z3	Anaerobi			

				c threshold			
	3	8x 400m	8x 400m				
	4	Z1	Z1				

Week 6

Resting Heart rate	KM	Tempo 10K with a smile	Heart rate zone for a PB	Average pace	Average heart rate	Average cadence
	7	Z3	Anaerobic threshold			
	3	5x 400m	5x 400m			
	4	Z1	Z1			

Week 7

Resting Heart rate	KM	Tempo 10K with a smile	Heart rate zone for a PB	Average pace	Average heart rate	Average cadence
	6	Z3	Anaerobic threshold			
	4	2x 2000m	2x 2000m			
	4	Z1	Z1			

Week 8

Resting Heart rate	KM	Tempo 10K with a smile	Heart rate zone for a	Average pace	Average heart rate	Average cadence

			PB			
	5	AT	AT			
	4	Z1	Z1			
	6	3x 2000m	3x 2000m			

Week 9

Resting Heart rate	KM	Tempo 10K with a smile	Heart rate zone for a PB	Average pace	Average heart rate	Average cadence
	7	Z3	Anaerobic threshold			
	4	4x 1000m	4x 1000m			
	5	Z1	Z1			

Week 10

Resting Heart rate	KM	Tempo 10K with a smile	Heart rate zone for a PB	Average pace	Average heart rate	Average cadence
	7	Z3	Anaerobic threshold			
	4	2x 2000m	2x 2000m			
	5	Z1	Z1			

Week 11

Resting Heart rate	KM	Tempo 10K with a smile	Heart rate zone for a PB	Average pace	Average heart rate	Average cadence

	7	Z3	Anaerobic threshold			
	6	3x 2000m	3x 2000m			
	5	Z1	Z1			

Week 12

Resting Heart rate	KM	Tempo 10K with a smile	Heart rate zone for a PB	Average pace	Average heart rate	Average cadence
	5	AT	AT			
	4	Z1	Z1			
	7	Z3	Anaerobic threshold			

Week 13

Resting Heart rate	KM	Tempo 10K with a smile	Heart rate zone for a PB	Average pace	Average heart rate	Average cadence
	8	Z3	Anaerobic threshold			
	6	6x 1000m	6x 1000m			
	5	Z1	Z1			

Week 14

Resting Heart rate	KM	Tempo 10K with a smile	Heart rate zone for a PB	Avg pace	Avg heart rate	Avg cadence
	8	AT	AT			
	12 minutes	10K pace	10K pace			
	12 minutes	10K pace	10K pace			
	10K RACE	Z3	**Anaerobic threshold**			

Interval Pace

10K time	Anaerobic threshold	2000m interval	1000m interval	400m interval	200m interval
30	3.09-3.04	7.00-6.30	3.23-3.08	1.15-1.09	34-31
31	3.15-3.10	7.12-6.42	3.29-3.14	1.17-1.11	35-32
32	3.21-3.16	7.24-6.54	3.35-3.20	1.19-1.13	36-33
33	3.27-3.22	7.36-7.06	3.41-3.26	1.22-1.16	37-33
34	3.33-3.28	7.48-7.18	3.47-3.32	1.24-1.18	38-33
35	3.39-3.34	8.00-7.30	3.53-3.38	1.26-1.20	38-34

36	3.45-3.40	8.12-7.42	3.59-3.44	1.29-1.23	39-35
37	3.51-3.46	8.24-7.54	4.05-3.50	1.31-1.25	40-36
38	3.57-3.52	8.36-8.06	4.11-3.56	1.33-1.27	41-36
39	4.03-3.58	8.48-8.18	4.17-4.02	1.36-1.30	42-37
40	4.09-4.04	9.00-8.30	4.23-4.08	1.38-1.32	43-38
41	4.15-4.10	9.12-8.42	4.29-4.14	1.40-1.34	44-48
42	4.21-.4.16	9.24-8.54	4.35-4.20	1.43-1.37	44-39
43	4.27-4.22	9.36-9.06	4.41-4.26	1.45-1.39	45-40
44	4.33-4.28	9.48-9.18	4.47-4.32	1.47-1.41	46-41
45	4.39-4.34	10.00-9.30	4.53-4.38	1.50-1.43	47-42
46	4.45-4.40	10.12-9.42	4.59-4.44	1.52-1.45	48-43
47	4.51-4.46	10.24-9.54	5.05-4.50	1.53-1.47	48-44
48	4.57-4.52	10.36-10.06	5.11-4.56	1.56-1.50	49-45
49	5.03-4.58	10.48-10.18	5.17-5.02	1.58-1.52	50-46
50	5.09-5.04	11.00-10.30	5.23-5.08	2.00-1.54	52-48
51	5.15-5.10	11.12-10.42	5.29-5.14	2.03-1.57	53-49
52	5.21-5.16	11.24-10.54	5.35-5.20	2.05-1.59	54-50
53	5.25-5.20	11.36-11.06	5.41-5.26	2.07-2.01	55-51

54	5.29-5.24	11.48-11.18	5.47-5.32	2.10-2.04	56-52
55	5.30	12.00-11.30	5.53-5.38	2.12-2.06	57-53
56	5.36	12.12-11.42	5.59-5.44	2.14-2.08	58-54
57	5.42	11.24-11.54	6.05-5.50	2.17-2.11	59-55
58	5.48	11.36-12.06	6.11-5.56	2.19-2.13	60-56
59	5.54	12.48-12.18	6.17-6.02	2.21-2.15	61-57
60	6.00	13.00-12.30	6.23-6.08	2.24-2.18	62-58
61	6.06	13.12-12.42	6.29-6.14	2.27-2.21	63-59
62	6.12	13.24-12.54	6.35-6.20	2.30-2.24	64-60
63	6.18	13.36-13.06	6.41-6.26	2.33-2.27	65-61
64	6.24	13.48-13.18	6.47-6.32	2.37-2.30	66-62
65	6.30	14.00-13.30	6.54-6.38	2.40-2.33	67-63

Chapter 9: Beginner schedules

In the beginning, running doesn't have to be fun at all. The runner's high and euphoric feeling that you sometimes hear runners talk about after running are not felt by most people after their first training. And that doesn't matter. Besides, after a week of running, you will not have all the positive effects that I discuss in this book. Don't get annoyed with yourself if you don't notice any positive effect after thirty minutes of running. Most of all, be happy that you did it. I like to compare it with cleaning your house. It's never fun to do, but once it's over, it's still enjoyable. I know people who have never experienced the runner's high after two years of running. So my advice to novice runners is not to look for euphoria or a good feeling, running injury-free and becoming more fit is the main goal.

No time

If you don't run that much yet, chances are you don't have enough time to run three times a week. That is a misunderstanding. Running does not take time, but it saves time. You will notice that you are simply going to do more in a single day. A 34-year-old woman once said that she always did household chores on Saturdays. The normal to-do list consists of getting groceries, ironing, washing, and cleaning. Her whole Saturday was consumed by these chores. Until she started training for a marathon and went for a run every Saturday at 8 a.m. After an hour of training, she drank a cup of coffee and took a shower. Then she did the household chores, and to her surprise, she finished before 13.00 every Saturday. She ran, and she won an entire afternoon to do things she liked doing. Anyone who starts running on a structural basis will notice this increase in productivity. So if you don't have time to run, go for a run.

Too tired to run? Go run

While sitting on the couch, never tell yourself that it is better not to run that day. Everyone can identify with it. You have worked hard for a day, and once you get home, you fall on the couch. You feel fatigued, and you think it is unwise to run; at least, you hope so. If you are too tired, you better rest, right? There is only one way to determine whether or not running is a good idea. Research has been conducted at the University of Maastricht into the predictive abilities of students in their running training. It turned out that students who had to predict at rest whether running was advisable could not do this properly. It turned out that they could only predict this after twelve minutes of running. So when you are tired (or have a cough), you should start running. If you are still limp and lifeless after twelve minutes, you can turn around and go home. But there is a good chance that you will enjoy it, and it does feel good.

Are you too heavy? Then cycle first

Being overweight is a good reason not to run. Of course, overweight people are often advised to exercise more in addition to a diet. Of course, I agree, but running if you are seriously overweight is asking for injuries. Your knee joints and tendons will have a hard time if you are overweight. In the table below I listed the boundaries between overweight that you can run well with and overweight that you shouldn't run with.

Length in cm	Length in ft in	Weight in KG	Weight in lbs	Weight in KG to run maximum of 35 minutes	Weight in lbs to run maximum of 35 minutes	Don't run above this weight in KG	Don't run above this weight in lbs
150	4 feet,	55	121.25	60	132.27	60	132.277

	11.06 in						
155	4 feet, 11.06 in	60.5	133.38	66	145.51	66	145.51
160	5 feet, 2.99 in	66	145.505	72	158.73	72	158.733
165	5 feet, 4.96 in	71.5	157.63	78	171.961	78	171.961
170	5 feet, 6.93 in	77	169.76	84	185.188	84	185.188
175	5 feet, 8.9 in	82.5	181.88	90	198.416	90	198.416
180	5 feet, 10.87 in	88	194.007	96	211.644	96	211.644
185	6 feet, 0.83 in	93.5	206.13	102	224.872	102	224.872
190	6 feet, 2.8 in	99	218.26	108	238.099	108	238.099
195	6 feet, 4.77 in	104.5	230.38	114	251.33	114	251.33

	in						
200	6 feet, 6.74 in	110	242.508	120	264.55	120	264.55
205	6 feet, 8.71 in	115.5	254.63	126	277.78	126	277.78

If you are in the left column, you can follow the beginner schedule without restrictions. Make sure that your running technique is good, especially if you are at the upper limit of the described weight.

If your weight is in the middle column, you can start following the beginner schedule, but you cannot run for more than 35 minutes. If you want to run for more than 35 minutes, you will need to lose weight. Don't be tempted by performance runs just yet because a knee injury can throw you far back in your build-up. First, run and lose weight, then build further over time.

If you are in the rightmost column, I strongly advise against running. You will probably be injured quickly after a good start, and that is a shame. I heartily recommend that you get started with your nutrition and go cycling or rowing. When you cycle or row, your weight is supported by a device, which saves your knee and hip joints. I also created a beginner schedule that starts with cycling or rowing. So you can still exercise injury-free.

These weights and advice apply to a reasonably good running technique. If you are not overweight and you follow the breathing advice in this book to monitor your limits, you can run injury-free. If you still suffer an injury, it is advisable to start running with a running coach to see if your technique can be improved. Never ignore knee and Achilles tendon aches because, once you overload them, you will most likely need a lot of rest, which will result in a fitness decline far worse than missing one training session.

They do lose weight, it is not fair

For runners, it is extremely demotivating and annoying if they do not lose weight. This irritation is intensified if someone else who has started running is already losing weight. The differences can be large, and comparing them with others makes no sense. It may very well be that two people who are both ten kilos (22 lbs) overweight start running together. If they both eat the same foods, run the same number of hours per week, and run in the same heart rate zone, they appear to be doing the same thing. Yet it is possible that one person will lose weight while the other does not. The table below explains why there can be a difference in weight loss. One runner can burn more calories during the same exercise than the other.

Power level	Maximum power in watt	Long endurance power in watt	Calories burned when training 3 times an hour a week in zone 3
Untrained	120	60	864
Average	140	70	1008
Good	160	80	1152
Sporty	200	100	1440
Very sporty	220	110	1584
Regional	240	120	1728
National	260	130	1872
International	300	150	2160
Worldclass	360	180	2592
Olympic medallist	400	200	2880

In the table above, you see different power levels with corresponding maximum powers (how strong someone is) and also the power that someone can deliver during a one-hour training session. Above is an example of someone who trains for an hour three times a week, 180 minutes a week. Also, you can see the number of calories burned in a week. You see that someone with a low maximum power uses fewer calories than someone with a "sporty" maximum power level.

So an athlete with a "normal" power level who runs in zone 3 will burn fewer calories than someone with a "very sporty" power level. This also means that as your fitness level increases, you will also burn more calories during the same workout. So do not be upset if you do not lose as much weight as you would like. Because it will get easier to burn more calories as your fitness level increases, if you follow the schedules described in this book.

The section above also reveals the formula for losing weight, which is incredibly simple. You will need to burn more calories than you take in.

If you want to discover how many calories you take in and how many you burn, you can follow my routine. I do this once in a while to make sure I am still on track. I like to begin with a rough estimate of how many calories I consume. I fill out all the foods and drinks I consume during a regular day in an app, to get a good estimate of my calorie intake. There are hundreds of apps available, so pick the one you like. Someone I coach, for instance, was shocked by how many calories he drank during a day, and by simply drinking less coffee, he was able to drastically lower his calorie intake, allowing him to lose weight. After you have discovered how many calories you take in. All you then need to know is how many calories you burn during an average day. Most smartwatches like a Garmin 245 can give you a great estimate, but you can also estimate it yourself via the hundreds of apps available and pick the one you like. Now that you know how many calories you take in and burn, you know whether you will be able to lose weight or if you need to change something. Remember to lose weight you need to burn more calories than you take in.

Other beginner schedules
In the beginning, it is advisable to build your average distance slowly to prevent injuries. However, try to run for at least 12 minutes at a time. If you run less than 12 minutes, your fitness gain will be minor, which is frustrating.

A lot of beginner schedules encourage you to run for one minute and then walk for one minute, etc. The disadvantage of this system is that your energy systems are not perfectly balanced as they are in heart rate zone 3.

In the first few minutes, you mainly use the readily available energy reserves in your muscles, which is the anaerobic energy system. As you learned before, this leads to a byproduct, acid. You are already out of balance, you rush your energy usage, and then you stop all at once. After the run, the body gets stuck in anaerobic energy consumption. If you are going to run for your health and to de-stress, this level is not useful. To improve your fitness, you need to run at an aerobic level, especially in the beginning. You also want to use your fat supply during your run. By running for short stretches and stopping after a minute, you won't do that.

I advise you to start with a 12-minute run. If 12 minutes of running is not possible, you can build up your fitness by cycling or rowing. As I've described below. Novice runners are sometimes shocked that I advise them to run for 12 minutes the first time. But it is good to realize that you do it at your own pace based on your heart rate as described by the schedule. Speed is not important. To run, you just need a "floating moment"; a moment when both legs are in the air, otherwise, you are walking. You can already have a "floating moment" at 7 to 8 km/h (4.34 to 4.97 mph), and most runners can also maintain that for 12 minutes in the beginning.

Schedule Beginner 5K
Week 1

Resting Heart rate	Minutes	Heart rate zone	Average pace	Average heart rate	Average cadence
	12	Z3			
	12	Z3			
	12	Z3			

Week 2

Resting Heart rate	Minutes	Heart rate zone	Average pace	Average heart rate	Average cadence
	14	Z3			
	14	Z3			
	14	Z3			

Week 3

Resting Heart rate	Minutes	Heart rate zone	Average pace	Average heart rate	Average cadence
	16	Z3			
	16	Z3			
	16	Z3			

Week 4

Resting Heart rate	Minutes	Heart rate zone	Average pace	Average heart rate	Average cadence
	18	Z3			
	18	Z3			
	18	Z3			

Week 5

Resting Heart rate	Minutes	Heart rate zone	Average pace	Average heart rate	Average cadence
	20	Z3			
	20	Z3			
	20	Z3			

Week 6

Resting Heart rate	Minutes	Heart rate zone	Average pace	Average heart rate	Average cadence
	22	Z3			
	22	Z3			
	22	Z3			

Week 7

Resting Heart rate	Minutes	Heart rate zone	Average pace	Average heart rate	Average cadence
	20	Z4			
	20	Z3			
	20	Z3			

Week 8

Resting Heart rate	Minutes	Heart rate zone	Average pace	Average heart rate	Average cadence
	22	Z4			
	22	Z3			
	22	Z3			

Week 8

Resting Heart rate	Minutes	Heart rate zone	Average pace	Average heart rate	Average cadence
	24	Z4			
	24	Z3			
	24	Z3			

Week 9

Resting Heart rate	Minutes	Heart rate zone	Average pace	Average heart rate	Average cadence
	26	Z4			
	26	Z3			
	26	Z3			

Week 10

Resting Heart rate	Minutes	Heart rate zone	Average pace	Average heart rate	Average cadence
	28	Z4			
	28	Z3			
	28	Z3			

Week 11

Resting Heart rate	Minutes	Heart rate zone	Average pace	Average heart rate	Average cadence
	30	Z4			
	30	Z3			
	30	Z3			

Week 12

Resting Heart rate	Minutes	Heart rate zone	Average pace	Average heart rate	Average cadence
	32	Z4			
	32	Z3			
	32	Z3			

Week 13

Resting Heart rate	Minutes	Heart rate zone	Average pace	Average heart rate	Average cadence
	34	Z4			
	34	Z3			
	34	Z3			

Week 14

Resting Heart rate	Minutes	Heart rate zone	Average pace	Average heart rate	Average cadence
	36	Z4			
	36	Z3			
	36	Z3			

Week 15

Resting Heart rate	Minutes	Heart rate zone for a PB	Heart rate zone running with a smile	Average pace	Average heart rate	Average cadence
	5K	Z4	Z3			

Training schedule for beginners that want to lose weight before they can run injury free

While cycling the anaerobic threshold is 10 beats lower, so correct your heart rate zones by simply subtracting 10.

Week 1

Resting Heart rate	Minutes	Heart rate zone	Sport	Average pace	Average heart rate	Average cadence
	20	Z3	Cycling			
	20	Z3	Cycling			
	20	Z3	Cycling			

Week 2

Resting Heart rate	Minutes	Heart rate zone	Sport	Average pace	Average heart rate	Average cadence
	22	Z3	Cycling			

	22	Z3	Cycling			
	22	Z3	Cycling			

Week 3

Resting Heart rate	Minutes	Heart rate zone	Sport	Average pace	Average heart rate	Average cadence
	24	Z3	Cycling			
	24	Z3	Cycling			
	24	Z3	Cycling			

Week 4

Resting Heart rate	Minutes	Heart rate zone	Sport	Average pace	Average heart rate	Average cadence
	26	Z3	Cycling			
	26	Z3	Cycling			
	26	Z3	Cycling			

Week 5

Resting Heart	Minutes	Heart rate	Sport	Average pace	Average heart rate	Average cadence

rate		zone				e
	28	Z3	Cycling			
	28	Z3	Cycling			
	28	Z3	Cycling			

Week 6

Resting Heart rate	Minutes	Heart rate zone	Sport	Average pace	Average heart rate	Average cadence
	30	Z3	Cycling			
	30	Z3	Cycling			
	30	Z3	Cycling			

Week 7

Resting Heart rate	Minutes	Heart rate zone	Sport	Average pace	Average heart rate	Average cadence
	12	Z3	Running			
	34	Z3	Cycling			
	34	Z3	Cycling			

Week 8

Resting	Minutes	Heart	Sport	Average pace	Average	Average

Heart rate	Minutes	rate zone	Sport	Average pace	Average heart rate	Average cadence
	14	Z3	Running			
	36	Z3	Cycling			
	36	Z3	Cycling			

Week 9

Resting Heart rate	Minutes	Heart rate zone	Sport	Average pace	Average heart rate	Average cadence
	16	Z3	Running			
	38	Z3	Cycling			
	38	Z3	Cycling			

Week 10

Resting Heart rate	Minutes	Heart rate zone	Sport	Average pace	Average heart rate	Average cadence
	18	Z3	Running			
	40	Z3	Cycling			
	40	Z3	Cycling			

Week 11

Resting Heart rate	Minutes	Heart rate zone	Sport	Average pace	Average heart rate	Average cadence

Resting Heart rate	Minutes	Heart rate zone	Sport	Average pace	Average heart rate	Average cadence
	14	Z3	Running			
	42	Z3	Cycling			
	42	Z3	Cycling			

Week 12

Resting Heart rate	Minutes	Heart rate zone	Sport	Average pace	Average heart rate	Average cadence
	16	Z3	Running			
	44	Z3	Cycling			
	44	Z3	Cycling			

Week 13

Resting Heart rate	Minutes	Heart rate zone	Sport	Average pace	Average heart rate	Average cadence
	22	Z3	Running			
	46	Z3	Cycling			
	22	Z3	Running			

Week 14

Resting Heart rate	Minutes	Heart rate zone	Sport	Average pace	Average heart rate	Average cadence
	24	Z3	Running			

| | 50 | Z3 | Cycling | | | |
| | 24 | Z3 | Running | | | |

Week 15

Resting Heart rate	Minutes	Heart rate zone	Sport	Average pace	Average heart rate	Average cadence
	26	Z3	Running			

Epilogue

I wrote this book with great pleasure, and I am happy to see that more people are running (marathons). I hope that I have inspired you, and I know that you will achieve all the goals you set. I am delighted that the demand for good personal schedules and injury-free running is increasing. Because more and more people want to run marathons, not everyone wants to use schedules that change their everyday lives considerably.

I hope this book contributes to responsible, and injury-free running. And it is my wish that many runners enjoy running and make progress with this book, even if they have never run before.

Because the beautiful feeling of running and making progress is something special. And I sincerely hope you will feel the same way. Not only for experienced runners, but also for those looking to lose weight or suffering from fatigue.

I dream of a more healthy world, and who knows, we may be able to give health care a push towards sports and relaxation.

Enjoy your running and may we meet again,

Would you be willing to leave a review on Amazon? And if you have feedback or questions you can get in touch with me via e-mail at runbyheartrate@gmail.com

References

Wellenkotter, J., Kernozek, T. W., Meardon, S., & Suchomel, T. (2014). The effects of running cadence manipulation on plantar loading in healthy runners. International journal of sports medicine, 35(09), 779-784.

Van Dyk, N., Behan, F. P., & Whiteley, R. (2019). Including the Nordic hamstring exercise in injury prevention programmes halves the rate of hamstring injuries: a systematic review and meta-analysis of 8459 athletes. British journal of sports medicine, 53(21), 1362-1370.

Le Marathon door F. Péronnet, G. Thibault, M. Ledoux, G. Brisson en Hermann.

Le Marathon door F. Péronnet, G. Thibault, M. Ledoux, G. Brisson en Hermann.

Powell KE, Kohl HW, Caspersen CJ, Blair SN. An Epidemiological Perspective on the Causes of Running Injuries. Phys Sportsmed. 1986 Jun;14(6):100-14.

Marti B, Vader JP, Minder CE, Abelin T. On the epidemiology of running injuries. The 1984 Bern Grand- Prix study. Am J Sports Med. 1988 May-Jun; 16(3): 285-94.

Brill PA, Macera CA. The influence of running patterns on running injuries. Sports Med. 1995 Dec;20(6):365-8.

Van Mechelen W. Running injuries. A review of the epidemiological literature. Sports Med. 1992 Nov; 14(5): 320-35.

Jacobs SJ, Berson BL. Injuries to runners: a study of entrants to a 10,000 meter race. Am J Sports Med. 1986 Mar-Apr; 14(2): 151-5.

Pollock ML, Gettman LR, Milesis CA, Bah MD, Durstine L, Johnson RB. Effects of frequency and duration of training on attrition and incidence of injury. Med Sci Sports. 1977 Spring; 9(1): 31-6.

Kluitenberg B, van der Worp H, Huisstede BM, Hartgens F, Diercks R, Verhagen E, van Middelkoop M. The NLstart2run study: Training-related factors associated with running-related injuries in novice runners. J Sci Med Sport. 2016 Aug;19(8):642-6

Principles of Exercise Testing and Interpretation: K. Wasserman, J. E. Hansen, D. Y. Sue e.a, uitgever Lippincott Williams and Wilkins

Milner, C. E.; Ferber, R.; Pollard, C. D.; Hamill, J.; Davis, I. S., Biomechanical Factors Associated with Tibial Stress Fracture in Female Runners. Medicine & Science in Sports & Exercise 2006, 38 (2), 323-328.

Moen, M. H.; Tol, J. L.; Weir, A.; Steunebrick, M.; De Winter, T. C., Medial tibial stress syndrome: a critical review. Sports Medicine 2009, 39 (7), 523-546.

Popp, K. L.; Hughes, J. M.; Smock, A. J.; Novotny, S. A.; Stovitz, S. D.; Koehler, S. M.; Petit, M. A., Bone Geometry, Strength, and Muscle Size in Runners with a History of Stress Fracture. Medicine & Science in Sports & Exercise 2009, 41 (12), 2145-2150.

Madeley, L. T.; Munteanu, S. E.; Bonanno, D. R., Endurance of the ankle joint plantar flexor muscles in athletes with medial tibial stress syndrome: A case-control study. Journal of Science and Medicine in Sport 2007, 10 (6), 356-362.

Madeley, L. T., Munteanu, S. E., & Bonanno, D. R. (2007). Endurance of the ankle joint plantar flexor muscles in athletes with medial tibial stress syndrome: a case-control study. Journal of Science and Medicine in Sport, 10(6), 356-362.

Printed in Great Britain
by Amazon